To

Thank you; and yes, are full of... stories!

Paul A Ficori

# On Grampus Ledge
## The Wreck of the Brig St. John on October 7, 1849

Paul A. Fiori

*AuthorHouse™*
*1663 Liberty Drive, Suite 200*
*Bloomington, IN 47403*
*www.authorhouse.com*
*Phone: 1-800-839-8640*

*© 2008 Paul A. Fiori. All rights reserved.*

*No part of this book may be reproduced, stored in a retrieval system, or transmitted by any means without the written permission of the author.*

*First published by AuthorHouse 11/17/2008*

*ISBN: 978-1-4389-3177-7 (sc)*

*Printed in the United States of America*
*Bloomington, Indiana*

*This book is printed on acid-free paper.*

# Acknowledgements And Thank You's

First of all I would like to thank the staffs of the Scituate Public Library, in Scituate, Massachusetts, the Hingham Public Library, in Hingham, Massachusetts, and the Paul Pratt Memorial Library in Cohasset, Massachusetts. They were more than gracious in granting me access to their stacks of books, and the use of their computers, and historical research areas.

Secondly, I would like to thank and acknowledge the staff of the Cohasset Historical Society. Without access to their mountainous archives on this wreck, this book does not get written properly. They answered all of my questions and guided me every step of the way, as this book took form, was molded and eventually completed in its current form.

A special debt of gratitude goes to Ed Brennock for steering me in the direction of his great-great grandfather, Michael Neptune Brennock, a medal recipient for rescue that sad October day.

A great deal of credit goes to E. Victor Bigelow, who wrote of the wreck in his *Narrative History of Cohasset: Volume One: Early Times to 1898*. However wonderful Bigelow's words were, no one described the situation in Cohasset days after the wreck better than Henry David Thoreau, in Chapter One of his book *Cape Cod*, entitled *The Shipwreck* a part of which I have quoted in this book.

Without the help of the St. John family the story of Mary Kane would not be complete. To Mr. and Mrs. Paul St. John, and their sons Mark, Brian, Brendan, and Martin, I say thank you!

Finally, to my family: to my children Jennifer, Anthony, and Krystin, and all of their friends, who have waited for me to finally complete a project – I did it! To my brothers Leo, Jr. and Jay, and my sister Tina, and their families; I hope you finally decide to read a book without pictures. To my brother Bob, whose knowledge of computers was invaluable at times of distress, and to his family; sorry I was such a pain in the ass!

To my Aunt Anne Fiori, and to my uncles Bruno and Dino and their families; I hope you all enjoy the book. To all my Rosano relatives now deceased: Aunt's Jo and Rosie, and my Uncles Saint, Pint, and Midgie; aka, Anthony, Frank, and Jimmy, rest in peace.

To my late mother, Mary (Rosano) Fiori, I miss you and love you. And finally to my dad, Leo J. Fiori, Sr., thanks for everything. I love you. Love to all of you, and Go Sox!

# Contents

CHAPTER ONE
    THE VISITOR      1

CHAPTER TWO
    THE TOWNS      4

CHAPTER THREE
    THE GREAT FAMINE      12

CHAPTER FOUR
    THE EMIGRATION ACTS      16

CHAPTER FIVE
    THE BRIG ST. JOHN      17

CHAPTER SIX
    THE STEPS      22

CHAPTER SEVEN
    THE VOYAGE      27

CHAPTER EIGHT
    CAPE COD      30

CHAPTER NINE
    BOSTON      34

CHAPTER TEN
    SCITUATE      37

CHAPTER ELEVEN
    COHASSET      39

CHAPTER TWELVE
    GRAMPUS LEDGE      41

CHAPTER THIRTEEN
    OCTOBER 8      50
    THE SEARCH      50

CHAPTER FOURTEEN
    "THE SHIPWRECK"      54

CHAPTER FIFTEEN
    FUNERAL AND MASSES:                              66
CHAPTER SIXTEEN
    THE CELTIC CROSS                                 69
CHAPTER SEVENTEEN
    QUESTIONS:                                       74
APPENDIX A
    REPORTS, DIARIES, AND NEWSPAPER ARTICLES ON
    THE WRECK OF THE ST. JOHN                        82
APPENDIX B
    PASSENGER LISTS AND CONFUSION                   121
APPENDIX C
    INTERVIEWS, LETTERS AND E-MAILS                 134
APPENDIX D
    POEMS                                           145

# CHAPTER ONE
## THE VISITOR

Cohasset, Massachusetts. St. Patrick's Day: 2007. A fresh mantle of snow covers the ground. It's not that light, fluffy January snow; it's March snow, heavy, lead-like, and moisture laden; the kind of snow that breaks backs when you shovel it – the kind of snow that causes heart attacks. It's ten in the morning and I'm on my way to Cohasset's Central Cemetery, also know as the Joy Place Cemetery.

I pass the Cohasset Historical Society: no one's home. Through the center of town now, past the Common; the 1st Parish Church is on my right; that's where two of the masses were held. Now the road dips, rises slowly, and veers to the left slightly. On my right is my destination. Turning now, I brake, and slip, and slide down a steep grade; the plows haven't done their work yet. I glide, slowly, hit the gas on a small rise, and come to a halt. There's an entrance to my right. Time to go, time to pay my respects.

Past the entrance and in; I'm walking, shuffling actually, through the newly fallen snow; it's slippery. Side stepping up a small hill, I stop. There it is, the reason I have come here today.

Standing atop this knoll is a 20-foot tall Celtic Cross, the symbol of Irish tenacity and will. It's made of granite, perhaps Cohasset granite, but most likely New Hampshire granite. Walking around the cross, I look up and down, checking out every inch of this stone memorial.

The cross is here in this old graveyard, to honor and keep alive the memory of the Forty-five mentioned, but more so, to the memory of the one hundred or more that rest in a watery grave a mile or so from this most hallowed ground.

It's quiet, most cemeteries are, or at least seem to be. It's not the silence of night; it's somehow different. Nighttime quiet can be broken

Paul A. Fiori

by the sound of a passing car, or footfalls; in a cemetery silence is different. I guess it can best be described as the silence of peace. There seems to be an absence of sound in a cemetery, of noise. Cemeteries are earth, and stone, and bone: all are still. The dead are calm in their rest, peaceful. There's a certain placidity here, a serenity, a tranquility. In silence, I read the inscription on the stone.

This cross was erected and dedicated to mark the final resting place of about forty-five Irish emigrants from a total company of 99 who lost their lives on Grampus Ledge off Cohasset, October 7, 1849, in the wreck of the Brig St. John, Galway, Ireland. R.I.P.

Now there is only a granite shaft to memorialize those who died that horrible day. Off shore, waves still crash over Grampus Ledge, and the Cohasset Rocks. That minefield of granite ledges has claimed many more ships and many more lives. Yet, here in this cemetery rest the hushed voices of the dead of the *St. John*, memorialized in stone, yet lying in an unmarked grave. Their spirits are restless and they dream dreams that will never die, and they hope eternally; their vision never dimmed. I hear a voice, if only in my mind, and it speaks to me.

"I am of the past, of days gone by and long forgotten; by some. I'm a ghost, an apparition, conjured up from the pages of some historical tome, written by an author unknown. I am here, now, to tell the truth, the whole story from start to finish. I'm a survivor, the spirit of one who died in that angry sea, on that granite-ledged Grampus, on that wild and harsh October morning, so many years ago. I was on that wheezing old ship, that ill-fated vessel. Fate, fickle as ever chose that I should die, that I should be placed in an unmarked grave with the others; now I'm back!

"I drift, I float, and I wander. I land safely, quietly, and unseen. Ah! Here it is our shrine where we, the dead, are memorialized forever. Alas! More granite! I touch it; yes, it's cool, as granite should be. I see no names, only the words of someone who never knew us, or what we were. I recall old friends, family, and neighbors; we all sailed on the *St. John*. All are gone now.

"We were so young then, so courageous, so adventurous. Planning our futures, looking for a new start in life after so much suffering. Now I wonder what might have been. Our hearts were strong, and we sailed with no regret, leaving family, friends, and the land we loved far behind – Erin! Oh Erin!

"We were so eager and filled with the zest for a new adventure. I, for one, could see it all in my mind; Boston, America, and the future. Now, here we are, at our rest 'neath the soil of a land few of ever set foot on alive. Our bodies found no safe haven here; yet our souls met with God."

# CHAPTER TWO
## THE TOWNS

Most of the information in this chapter was gleaned from the Clare County Library website at, www.clairelibrary.ie, and from *The Parliamentary Gazetteer of Ireland, 1845*, at the same website.

It was a land of hunger and strife. Ireland had for years, been caught in the clutching hand of *An Gorta Mor*: The Great Hunger. Thousands had perished, and entire families ceased to exist. Most people stayed and endured their suffering; those who could, left.

They came from County Clare and County Galway, in southwestern Ireland. From towns and parishes whose names seem to roll easily off the tongue of someone equipped with a irish brogue, or who spoke the music of Gaelic: Clare, Ennis, Ennistymon, Dysart, Lahinch, Ruan, Galway, Connemara, Lettermullen and Kilmurry, towns that bordered the Atlantic Ocean and the Burren, that lunar-like landscape of Dolmens and burial chambers, where wolves prowl and bears are hunted.

The Burren occupies an area of over 100 square miles in the northern part of County Clare. It is, more or less, a limestone-encrusted plateau. Scenic, yet barren, author Edmund Ludlow, described it thusly, and I quote. "There is not water enough to drown a man, wood enough to hang one, nor earth enough to bury him."

From this flat, desert-like plateau, one may escape, within a few miles, to verdant vales and hills, rich in bramble and hazel. Here, the winds that blow off the Atlantic howl incessantly.

County Clare, in the Province of Munster, is a maritime county. To the west lies the Atlantic, to the NW is Galway Bay, and running SE is the River Shannon. *Tuath Mumhanor,* or North Munster, came into being early on. This area was ruled by the Clans O'Brien, O'Connor, O'Dea, O'Garbh, O'Laughlin, McMahan, and McNamara.

It isw a beautiful area, with many a sheltered bay and sandy beach. The Bridges of Ross were naturally formed by storm waves beating into the rocks and forming natural arches. Loop Head has some interesting and unusual rock formations also. Blackhead, a coastal road, passes between the Atlantic on one side, and the Burren on the other. The Cliffs of Moher are also found here.

East Clare is different, offering a more gentle and relaxed landscape, with numerous lakes and streams. The River Shannon and Lough Deng are found here.

County Clare was greatly affected by the famine. Between 1845-1850 over 50,000 people died and 74,000 emigrated from this area.

In Gaelic, it can be spoken several ways: *Clar,* meaning, perhaps, board or wooden bridge; or *Droichead an Chlair, Claradard a Chordah, Clar-atha-da-Chordah,* which in English names the town Clare, or Clare Abbey.

Clare is in County Clare, in the Barony of Islands, in Munster Province. It is two miles south of Ennis, on the River Fergus, on the Ennis-Limerick Road. The town took its name from Clare Castle.

It is an area of good land. On the way to Ennis and along the banks of the Fergus, lay the ruins of Clare Abbey, built in 1194. In 834, there were 100 Protestants and 4,100 Catholics in this small town.

Those on the *St. John* from Clare included, Honora Lahiff, John Lahiff, Honora Mulkennan and Margaret Mulkenan.

Ennis, or in gaelic, *Innis,* is on the banks of the River Fergus, at the confluence of the Clareen. It is in the parish of Drumcliffe, Barony of Islands, County Clare, and Munster Province. This town is 7 miles SSE of Corrofin, 15 miles SSw of Gort, 18 miles from Limerick, 24 miles W of Killaloe, and over 100 miles from Dublin. It is the capital of County Clare.

*Paul A. Fiori*

The River Fergus, while lending a pastoral setting to the area, is hardly beautiful but adds more than the swamps and bogs found nearby. The area does have some pleasant features however, but it is, more often than not, bleak, cold, and rock-bound. A rocky plain stretches from the banks of the Fergus, to the head of Galway Bay, and over to Lough Rea, and Oranmore. The town's original name may have been *Innischan-Ruadha*.

Those on board from Ennis included, Mary Freeman and child, a Mr. Egan and his wife and daughter.

Ennistymon, or *Inni Diomain, Inis na Mhun, Innis Diamain*, in Gaelic, meaning "Diamain's Riverside Meadow," or even "Island of the Middle House," or yet again, "Fruitful Riverside Meadow," or maybe "Diamain's Island," is the name of a river and a town.

The River Ennistymon flows west and is found in County Clare, Munster Province, and forms the boundary between the Baronies of Ibrickane and Islands, then flows across the Barony of Inchiquin, forming the boundary between the baronies of Inchuquin and Corcomroe. The river rolls on for 16 miles, through Ennistymon and into Liscannor Bay.

The town is found in the Parish of Kilmanaheen, Barony of Corcomroe, County Clare, and Munster Province. It is 2 miles E of Liscanor Bay, 8 miles NE of Miltown-Malbay, 9 miles W of Corofin, 13 miles WNW of Ennis, and 125 miles SW of Dublin. It is on the River Ennistymon.

Thee is a romantic feel to this town, as the river glides gently by, only to leap joyously over high, broken crags, and ledges, forming a fall and rapids as beautiful to the eye and ear, as anything similar on this island country.

From Ennistymon came Bridget Quinn, Eliza O'Brien, Ann Slattery, Bridget Slattery, Hugh Madigan, Margaret Keenan, Hugh Glynn, Margaret Keenan, and a Miss Brooks.

The parish of Dysart, also called Dyset, or, in gaelic, *Disert*, is in the Barony of Inchiquin, County Clare, and Dysart Parish, in Munster Province. It is 4.5 miles from Ennis, on the Corofin Road.

It is a wild country, with few inhabitants. The land is, for the most part, mountainous, rock strewn, and far from profitable; there is barely any arable land. Its western border is formed by the River Fergus and its rivulets, which flow west, and into the Atlantic. Small loughs add depth to an otherwise cold and barren landscape. There are numerous castles, but they are as boring in structure and design as the land they lord over. In 1834 there were 65 Protestants and 1,700 Catholics in Dysart.

From Dysart came Martin Sexton, James Moran, and Jeremiah Murphy.

Kilfenora, or in Gaelic, *Cill Fhinnurach*, is the name of a parish and a town. It is located on the south side of the Burren, in the Barony of Corcomroe, County Clare, Munster Province. To the south is Lough Lakeen, and further south is Slievebeg. This is an area of prime farmland.

There have been numerous translations of its gaelic name, including: "Church of the Fertile Hillside, Church of the White Meadow, and Church of the Fair White Brow." Kilfenora is also known as the "City of the Seven Crosses." In the past the town has gone by the names: Fenbore, Finneborasis, Kilfenoragh, and Cellumbrach. In 1846, there were 700 Protestants and 3,000 Catholics in town. The Catholic mass was said at St. Facanan's.

From Kilfenora came Patrick Lahiff, John Lahiff, Thomas Riley, and Bridget Madigan.

Kilmury-Clondrlaw, Kilmury-Ibrickane, and Kilmury-Negaul, left me in a quandary. I found that Kilmury-Negaul suited my purposes best: so much for the confusion.

The town of Kilmury is in the Parish of Kilmury-Negaul, in the Barony of Upper Tulla; but was moved to the Barony of Lower Bunratty in 1845, in County Clare, Munster Province. It is fine, arable farmland. The town is 2 miles NW of the colorfully named town of Sixmilebridge, on the Quinn Road. In 1834 there were 5 Protestants and 700 Catholics in town.

From this town came: Mary Flannagan/Hannagan, Nancy Flannagan/Hannagan, Margaret Flannagan/Hannagan, Patrick Lahiff,

John Lahiff, Thomas Riley, Bridget Maddigan, Patrick McGrath, James McGrath, Winny Galvin, Margaret Kane, and Mary McNamara.

Lahinch, or *An Leacht, or Leath Innis*, meaning "The Half Island," is located in the Barrony of Corcomroe, Kilmanaheen Parish, Kilmacreahy, County Clare, Munster Province. It rests at the head of Liscanor Bay. The Atlantic is to the west, the River Innagh to the north, and the River Mayo to the south, on the Miltown-Malbay Road. It is 2 miles WSW of Ennistymon. Lahinch is known for its beaches and bathing areas. Nearby are the curiousities known as the Puffing Holes and the Dripping Well. The town was once known as *Leacht O'Croixixhubhare*, or O'Connor's cairn."

From Lahinch came Michael Flannagan/Hannagan, Daniel Byrnes, Ellen Hasset, Michael Griffen, Catherine Burnes, and Peggy Molloy.

*An Ruan*, meaning "Alder Tree," is the Gaelic form of Ruan. This town is in County Clare, the Barony of Inchiquin, and Dysart Parish, in Munster Province. Ruan lies on the edge of the Burren, and close to Dromar Lough. It is 3.5 miles from Corofin, and 7 miles north of Ennis.

From Ruan came Bridget McMahan, Patrick McMahan, Catherine McMahan, Mary Nalon, and Mary Frowley and her child.

County Galway is bordered by the Atlantic on the west, on its north by Mayo and Roscommon, to the east by Roscommon, King's County, and Tipperary, and on the south by County Clare and Galway Bay.

Five thousand years ago, the Celts found their way into what would become County Galway. It has a rich, yet varied landscape. Filled with legend and lore, it is one of the most beautiful areas of Ireland. It is the second largest county in Ireland, only County Cork is larger. It is found in the Province of Connaught.

It is an area teeming with monasteries, built at the dawn of Christianity. Fine examples of early Celtic monasteries can be found at Lough Corrib, Annaghdown, and the Isle of Inchaquill.

Galway Bay, or *Cuan na Gaillimhe*, is tucked between West Galway, and the northern edge of County Clare. The bay is 30 miles in length, and varies from 7-20 miles in width. On the way out of the Galway harbor and into the bay, you will pass the Twelve Bens and the Aran Islands.

"The Stony River," *Gaillimh*, or Galway City, is in County Galway, Province of Connaught, on Ireland's west coast. The River Corrib runs through it, as it winds its way to Galway Bay.

It is the only city in the Province of Connaught, and the capital of County Galway. The earliest settlement here was called *Dun Bhun na Gaillimhe*, or "Fort at the bottom of the stony river."

Sailing from Galway were Patrick Corman, Miles Sweeney, Bridget Burke, Thomas Burke, Eliza Burke, Mary McDermott, Joyce McDermott and child, Catherine Fitzpatrick, Peggy Purky, John Belton, Mary Dolan, Thomas Fahey, Bridget Fahey, Martha Fahey, Honora Donnelly, Honora Mullen, Catherine Heniff, ?? Heniff, Mary Cahill, Patrick Noonan, Mary Landsky, Meggy Mullen and her sister's child, and John Butler.

*Ali Clochan*, or Connemara, is located in the western part of County Galway, between Lough Corrib and the Irish coast, to the north of Galway Bay. It is wild and barren country, a patchwork quilt of bogs, loughs, mountains and vales. On its coast are sandy bays and beaches, which rest quietly below craggy and too dangerous cliffs. Atop these cliffs lie flatlands, which melt into low-lying hills, isolated peaks and valleys, that enclose her black-watered loughs.

From Connemara came Bridget Connelly, Patrick Sweeney, his wife and eleven children.

In Gaelic, *Leiter Mellain*, Lettermullen is a small island located off the west coast of Ireland, near Connemara, County Galway, Ireland; it is about thirty miles from Galway City. It is the westernmost of three islands: Lettermullen, Lettermore, and Tin an Fhia, collectively known as Gorumna. It is now connected to the mainland via bridges and causeways. The islands are part of the Gaeltacht Region. In this region Gaelic is the main language spoken. From this tiny island came the Flaherty Brothers.

Prior to 1845, the residents of these and other Irish towns and parishes were happy, and would barely entertain the thought of leaving their homeland; even though they were at the beck and call of their English landlairds, ruled by unfair laws, and were persecuted for being Catholic, they stayed. They were farmers. However, in 1845, things changed drastically with the onset of *An Gorta Mor*, "The Great Hunger."

As an example of how bad things were in Ireland at that time, we will look at the Ennistymon Workhouse records, from July 31, 1849- September 1, 1849, prior to the sailing of the brig *St. John*. Then we will take a short look at *An Gorta Mor*.

A look at the Ennistymon Workhouse records for July 31, 1849, shows that there were ten new cases of fever, ten of dysentery, five of measles, and one new case of cholera. Seven people died of either fever, dysentery, or diarrhea. One person died of cholera, and one from measles. At this time, there were 98 people in the treatment in Ennistymon, and 60 at the Lahinch Auxillary.

On August 4, there were eight new cases of fever, ten of dysentery, four of measles, and one new case of chicken pox. At the same time, the Lahinch Auxiliary was treating %9 New cases. There were deaths at Lahinch from various maladies. At Ennistymon, there were three deaths from fever, three from measles, two from dysentery, and one from cholera.

Ten days later, there were fifty people in the fever hospital in Ennistymon, and seventy in its infirmary. In that time-span, there were six new cases of fever. In Ennistymon, nine more people died, twenty more died at Lahinch. By August 16, there were four new cases of fever, three new cases of diarrhea, two of dysentery, one of dropsy, and one of measles.

By August 21, there were sixty-eight people in the infirmary and twenty-two in the fever hospital there were also four new cases of fever. Four people died in Ennistymon, three died in Lahinch. The deaths were due to fever, chicken pox, diarrhea, dysentery, measles, dropsy, and one person died from convulsions.

One week later, on August 28, there are sixty-one people in the infirmary and twenty-eight in the fever hospital. This was a mild week in retrospect. There were only nine new cases and only six deaths, two of the deaths being in Lahinch. These deaths were due to dysentery, diarrhea, and measles.

By the time the brig *St. John* was ready to sail, September 5, 1849, there were fifty-nine cases in the infirmary and thirty more in the fever hospital. There were one hundred and forty three people being treated at the Lahinch Auxiliary alone. From 1847-1849, there were an estimated 3,000 deaths in County Clare, alone; is it any wonder these people wanted a new life elsewhere?

# CHAPTER THREE
## THE GREAT FAMINE

Volumes have been written on the subject of The Great Hunger, The Great Famine, The Potato Blight, or whatever you choose to call it. Most people have heard of it, and some have read at length about it. Not wanting to cover the subject in-depth, for I could probably go in endlessly on those famine-ridden years, I will give you, the reader, just a short glimpse at that wretched time; the years that changed the face of Ireland forever.

The Famine was probably the main reason for the mass exodus of people emigrating from Ireland to places like Australia, England, Canada, and the United States. However, it was not the only reason. A depressed English economy, religious persecution and maltreatment at the hands of their English landlairds and the English government, along with the blight, were reason enough to flee the lush, green island, in search of a new and better life.

Prior to 1845, when the blight first set in, there were an estimated 8.2 million relatively happy and healthy people living in Ireland. There were tradesmen: weavers, coopers, and saddlers; farmers: dairy and soil; fishermen; professional people: doctors and lawyers, and many others. The weavers of Ulster spun wool, or linen, from flax; linen was the largest export from Ulster, and its linen known worldwide. Coopers made barrels and staves; saddlers made sure you rode your horse in comfort, and tanners turned hide into beautiful leather. The farmers raised cows, sheep, lamb and pigs; they sold milk and cream also. Those who chose to farm the land chose as their main product, the potato. However, the potato was difficult to transport, in some ways; they could be heavy and awkward. They could be stored for up to eight months, at which point they rotted. The potato was destined to become the main food source for many poor Irish. When the blight hit, an Irish family of five was consuming 200 lbs. of potatoes per week. From 1845-1850, over one million people would leave Ireland forever, due in part to the failure of the potato crop.

In 1845, phytophthora infestans, a type of fungus, attacked Ireland's potato crop. Fungal spores carried over on the Atlantic winds, from North America, arrived in silence. These infestans, or fungi, hit the leaves of the potato plants and then slowly spread through the whole plant: leaf, stem, and root. There was no mistaking a diseased plant: the leaves are dead and withered, and black spots and white mold can be seen on the potato itself, before turning the potato into nothing more than a ball of mush. In the strange way that nature works, this disease affected no other crop. One-third to one-half of the 1845 potato crop was ruined, and the price of potatoes soared, doubling before the new year. By the end of 1845, 58,538 people had left Ireland.

1846 dawned new and full of hope; there would be no relief. This year the entire crop was wiped out! Starvation ensued; people were actually eating grass, roots, or leaves, anything they felt might be edible; anything that might relieve their suffering. Disease ran rampant: fever, dysentery, and cholera, By the time the blight had run its course many people would die from these and other diseases. If those living in the country were suffering mightily, those living in the city had it a bit easier, since they had access to fresher imported food products. The area hit hardest by the blight was the western part of the island, especially Connaught and Munster Provinces. Most of those who would be sailing on the *St. John*, in 1849, were from Munster Province. By the end of 1846, another 82,239 people had left Ireland; some sailed for Boston.

Now there was mass starvation. Their English landlairds were evicting thousands of starving families. Many of these families will end up living in scalpeens: hovels dug into the side of a hill.

People are homeless, sick, and weak. The London government will not lift a hand to help. The Irish are pleading for grain to use as a supplement; the government refuses to send them any; the Irish ask for money, with the same result. Their landlairds turned the land the Irish once farmed into dairy farms, very profitable dairy farms too. The workhouses are full; as nearly 750,000 poor are now being fed from state sponsored soup kitchens. Private charities try their best to assist; the Quakers help out, as do Catholic charities, and Protestant ministers; the blight you see, knows no religion. Friends, family, and strangers in America donate money, as do English businessmen; Queen Victoria donates 25,000 pounds to the Irish cause. Clothing arrives by the ton, to replace the disease-ridden rags many are suffered to wear. While the importation of food is substantial it cannot relieve everyone's suffering. By the middle of June, 2.5 million Irish are being fed by the state. There are food wars at state-run soup kitchens. A rumor is spreading all over Ireland that states, if you convert to the Church of England, you will be fed.

C.E. Trevelyan was the English Treasury secretary in charge of, or the person most involved with Irish famine relief. Trevelyan was of the belief that feeding the poor and famished of Ireland could only result in an increase in that sector of the Irish population, "… they fornicate like bunnies!" he'd say. To Trevelyan that only meant more Irish mouths to feed.

Trevelyan would write in early 18446, and I quote. "…the over-population of Ireland, being altogether beyond the power of man, the cure has been applied by the direct soul of an all-wise Providence (God) in a manner as unexpected and as unthought of as it is likely to be effectual."

Later that same year he would write, "…the great evil with which we have to contend is not the physical evil of the famine, but the moral evil of the selfish, perverse and turbulent character of the Irish people." Trevelyan would later be knighted for his work for the Irish.

In England, Prime Minister Peel defies everyone by ordering that the corn sent from America be sent to the starving Irish. Peel organizes work programs. He tries to change the Work Laws, and did all in his power to help the Irish. In the next elections, Peel was soundly defeated. The new Prime Minister, Lord Russell, put an end to all of Peel's good work. In 1847, 142,154 more people leave Ireland.

By 1848, things improved as much as they remained the same. Families that had left Ireland, and were settled elsewhere, began to send money back to Ireland. Some of those receiving this welcomed gift would use it to improve their lot; others would save and save, until they had enough for passage to a new and better land.

Now, Three million are being fed in the soup kitchens. Workhouses are filled to capacity, thousands are dying everyday, and mass graves become an accepted norm.

By mid-summer, the blight has returned from its short hiatus. Once more entire crops are wiped out. The death rate is escalating. Many are dying from weakness due to malnutrition. Cholera rears its ugly and deadly head, once more. By June of 1849, 188,233 new emigrants had left Ireland; some had their trips paid for by the landlairds who just wanted them anywhere but on Irish soil.

By the time 1849 came to a close, another 219,450 Irish will sail away; included in that number will be those who chose to sail onboard the British brig *St. John*. It is now September 5, 1849: the brig *St. John* is preparing to sail.

Now the Voice speaks in questions. "How cruel is the nation, and its controlling hand, that expels one person, or one family from their land? How cruel is the landowner that ousts a family, because it is cheaper for *him* that way? How sad is the farmer who toiled, who labored, and sweat daily to feed the well-to-do, while his own family suffered and wailed on empty stomachs? Why would those, so mighty and grand, so filled with beef and grain, sit by idly and watch their fellow man suffer and die? Only they can answer these questions of mine.

"With head bowed, heart-broken, and of shattered spirit, we and our children visit a grave. Tears fall and hands are clutched. Your love is gone, now and forever. It might be your wife, or husband, your son or daughter, their mother or father, their sister or brother. One last look; farewell, and a last kiss good-bye."

# CHAPTER FOUR
## THE EMIGRATION ACTS

The English Poor Laws held that English landlairds were responsible for paying the taxes for any of their tenants living on lands worth four pounds or less. Many of the landlairds simply evicted their tenants in order to reduce the amount of tax the had to pay. This forced many Irish to leave their homeland. For a fortunate few, their former landlairds gratefully paid their passage to wherever they chose to go.

For those emigrants that did not have the money for the fare to their chosen destination, there were two other types of assistance available to them: Emigrant Remittances, and Poor Law Assisted Emigration.

Emigration remittances were monies received from relatives who were already settled elsewhere; this may have applied to some of those sailing on the *St. John*. The money was saved and when enough for passage was accrued it was sent back to family in Ireland, in hopes that those receiving it would soon join them.

Poor Law Assisted Emigration was made up of two distinct sections: an Orphan Emigration section, which may or may not have pertained to anyone on the *St. John*, and a General Emigration section. The second section had been put forth by the English government in 1849, in order to lessen the burden at Ireland's overcrowded workhouses. This plan helped the English Board of Guardians to clear the workhouses, and sent many Irish to new places. This is how it worked.

If a person, or persons were thought to be fit for work by the Board of Guardians, and they had been residing at a workhouse for more than a year, they were deemed eligible to receive this form of assistance. Many able-bodied Irish made it to America, or other countries this way.

# CHAPTER FIVE
## THE BRIG ST. JOHN

The great ship these nervous yet excited Irish folk were about to sail into the future upon, was the British brig *St. John*. A brig is a ship with two masts, with one of the masts being square-rigged. A square-rigged mast is a four-cornered sail suspended from yardarms and carried on either, a square-rigged, or fore-and-aft rigged ship. The *St. John* weighed 200 tons; others state that she was a full-rigged ship weighing 985 tons. She was an Irish-owned vessel, but of British registry.

Another story has the ship as being a 140' long, brig, full-rigged, and three-masted. Built as a passenger ship, she also carried cargo on the Liverpool-to-Boston route. She was owned by Owens & Company of Liverpool, and built in St. John, New Brunswick, Canada.

There are many opinions as to where the *St. John* was built. According to some she was built in the 1820's in Claddagh, Galway, County Galway, Ireland, by Master Shipwright, Toona O'Canaola, of Lettermullen, County Galway, Ireland.

O'Canaola was her first master. Her maiden voyage being made to St. John, New Brrunswick, where, it is said, she acquired her name. From that maiden voyage until the September day she set sail for Boston, she had made hundreds of successful voyages.

However, according to Lt. Cmdr. Niall Brunicardi, of Fermoy, County Cork, Ireland, the *St. John*, a full-rigged ship, had as her master, at one time, a fellow named Richardson. This story has the ship being built in St. John, New Brunswick, Canada, in 1844. Its owner being Owens & Company, of that same port.

Another story is told by "Paddy" Mulkerrin. "Paddy" says the ship was built in Galway, on a date unknown, by Tony Conneely of

Lettermullen. The money to build her come from Conneely's brother, an Anglican minister. Her owner was Tony Conneely – it is my opinion that no mater how it is spelled, Mr. Conneely is one and the same person (this is in regards to the spelling of both his first and last names: Toona or Tony, Conneely or O'Canaola). Mulkerrin's also states that Conneely was supposed to have sailed the ship to Boston, but his wife took ill and was replaced by Oliver. Others say that it was a Captain Greene that took ill. Captain Oliver was from Bohermore, County Galway. Another report states that the ship was owned by Mr. Henry Comerford, of Ballykeale House, Kilfenora, County Galway, Ireland.

With an increasing amount of emigrant travel, changes were bound to come. Early on, the ships used were more often than not broken down freighters, in such bad shape that they couldn't be counted on to deliver a cargo of valuable goods safely. These old, and for the most part unseaworthy vessels were refitted, with every available inch of space to be used for bunks for their new cargo – human beings! Many, if not most, of these vessels would filled beyond the limits of safety. American ships in the same business were held to a much higher standard.

Attached to the *St. John*, as on all ships were two smaller craft, a jollyboat and a longboat. The jollyboat was attached to the ships stern. Such a boat was often used by a ships crew in the performance of general duties, and is more often used as a tender, or a scout boat. Such a craft is best used in waters that are sheltered, such as harbors, or rivers, and is used to transport people to shore. Usually about 18' long and 8' wide, with a draft of 20', a jollyboat has a squared stern and can be propelled by oar or sail. It is a lot like a pinnance, a small, light craft, generally two-masted and schooner-rigged.

The longboat is larger than a jollyboat; it is usually 25'-30' long. It is an open boat, rowed by 8-10 oarsmen. It is a relative to the cutter, with finely defined lines to aft, which permits its use in rough seas, or winds blowing against the tide. Its beam is similar to that of a cutter, but broader than that of a gig. More seaworthy than a cutter, a longboat has less of a stern.

## On Grampus Ledge

The politically correct will call the *St. John* an immigrant ship. Historians might call her a famine ship. Those who sailed to Boston on her might refer to her as a coffin ship. Call it what you may, this is how she was planned out.

As on most ships of the time, her lowest deck was the storage deck. This was used to store baggage, the ship's food, and any goods being transported to the next port. Above this deck was the steerage deck; this is also a passenger deck. Above this was the cabin, or first deck. This also held passengers, as well as quarters for the captain and the crew.

The passengers in steerage paid the minimum fare for the voyage to America; usually 3 pounds, 10 shillings, or about $4.50 apiece. Though this may seem like a relatively small price to pay, it was nearly half a years pay for many poverty-stricken Irish. Ninety percent of the passengers on the *St. John* rode in steerage. Those that rode in the cabins paid 5-8 pounds to do so. Three of the ship owners' nieces were in the cabin.

The better, perhaps safer ships had only one immigrant deck. Others had two or even three. That third deck, located in the bowels of the ship was, in all honesty – a hell hole! Many times these shit-holes of a ship were undermanned, so much so, that in a howling storm at sea the male passengers might be called to do the work of a sailor. Food, or what passed for it was often in short supply, and the passengers had to supply their own. After paying for their voyage, many of the passengers had little or no money to purchase supplies from the ship's meager offerings, those unfortunates had to rely on the charity of their fellow passengers. They had to do their own cooking on the small stoves, or grates, located on the open deck. Lines were always long since only a scant few could use the cooking area at the same time. The ill, and at times there were many, had to rely on the kindness of family or friends to get their food to them.

Fortunately, for some, they were allowed to bring for themselves and their families, their own food, to supplement the ship's fare. A passenger was allowed 3 quarts of water for daily use, 2 1/2 lbs, of bread or biscuits, 1 lb. of wheat flour, 5 lbs. of oatmeal, and 2 lbs. of rice. In addition, a passenger could bring aboard 2 oz. of tea leaves, ½ lb. of sugar, 1 gallon of molasses, and 5 lbs. of potatoes, which could be substituted for the oatmeal or rice.

British Maritime Law stated, at the time, that the ship's owner must provide 7 lbs. of food per week, per passenger, plus an adequate supply of water for all on board a ship. Often this amount was less, and sadly, the food when provided was hardly edible. The food wasn't cooked properly and consisted mainly of salt fish, or salt meal, and maggot-infested meal. Because of the shortage of fresh water, most passengers refused to eat the salted foods because they knew they'd never be able to quench their thirst afterwards.

The ship's fresh water supply was stored in old, musty casks, or kegs, stored below decks; the water was always served warm. Often the casks leaked and prior to being purchased by the ship's owner may have been used to store wine or beer, which made the water undrinkable to many. The 3 ½ qts. of water given a person per day, had to used for drinking, cooking, and washing, which was virtually impossible to do; and what might the result of such an existence be?

Disease! The beds, or what passed for beds, were filthy, bug-infested, and were never brought out on deck to air or be cleaned. The floors in steerage were never cleaned, scraped, or washed in any way, to prevent the spread of disease; I won't even discuss the john's, or the areas near them. In some cases malnutrition set in, teeth fell out, and gums swelled up, turning sponge-like. People endured all of this, and more, just for that chance at a new life.

During the crossing you have hundreds of people, strangers for the most part, huddled together, without proper light, wallowing, like pigs in a sty, breathing, if they couldn't get out on deck, the fetid air of steerage, all day and all night. Space for sleeping was so tight that it was virtually impossible to get comfortable. Small bunks were built onto the walls of the steerage deck, and there were bunks on the floor as well, cramping conditions even more. One bathroom had to suffice for the one hundred plus in steerage; if you were lucky enough to gain access to the john, you often had uninvited guests – rats

Since I do not have any information in regards to the ages of all of the passengers on board the *St. John*, I'm going to say that most of the passengers were young Irish men and women, some with children, in their mid to late twenties; again this is just a guess. There may have been about twenty-six children on board; again, this is just a supposition. We do know that there were at least seventeen children on board.

The passengers were bound for Boston and a new life. They were escaping *An Gorta Mor*, and their landlairds, leaving their families behind in some cases. The date of departure was near. As she bobbed patiently in the still waters of Galway bay, the squat, slow brig, with its aging timbers, awaited her passengers. The *St. John* has been described as "none to seaworthy. An ancient craft, one of the untrustworthy hulks used in conveying Irish immigrants on the hazardous passage to North America…" Others would state, "She cannot be proven to be unseaworthy…" She was carrying in ballast, limestone.

British law was lax when it came to immigrant ships, such as the *St. John*. These famine or coffin ships, would be stuffed way beyond capacity; such was the case of the *St. John*. According to Captain Oliver, there were 100 passengers and 16 crew on board when she left Galway. This number would change at Lettermullen where Oliver let 50-60 more passengers on board – and the debate rages on to this day.

# CHAPTER SIX
## THE STEPS

The *St. John* is about to sail, and again I hear the Voice speak. "It is a beautiful day, enchanting for September. Overhead I hear gulls singing out joyously, and a light breeze comes up and answers them. The harbor is still, as waves roll to shore and gently lap and kiss; teasingly, pleasingly, with their ebb and their flow.

"We are preparing to leave now, leaving the Land of Erin. Many of us have had our spirits broken, snapped like a dead twig. However, we will recover; it's the Irish way. Fears must be dispelled, to be replaced by hope; hope, you see, is our savior, faith is our grace, as we set out for the future; that great unknown. As I wait, I think, and a single tear cuts through the map of Ireland, that I wear as a mask.

"Is this land that I love, this Erin, so evil that it has chased us away? We'd worked here, and struggled. We'd loved here, had husbands, wives, sons, and daughters, and now we are leaving. We cried out when hungry, and moaned and wept at death, and those of us here today just watch as our ship is being loaded with goods, and a soon to be human cargo.

"We stopped at graves, we wept and prayed and bade Godspeed to loved ones; we are all but babes in the arms of the Lord. Now it is time to board and bid farewell to Erin."

Before leaving Ireland forever, the passengers had to pass through six steps, or phases. They are: paying for their passage, a medical inspection, embarkation, departure, a search for stowaways, and lastly, roll call. Here is a quick, yet hopefully informative look at these phases, or steps. The first and most obvious step, for those who did not have their passage paid in advance, is to pay the fare.

The dock, or quay, is filled with anxious passengers, and over-zealous passenger brokers (that times version of a travel agent). Both parties haggle over the price, each trying to make the best deal for themselves. The competition among passenger brokers is fierce, as prices change daily, hourly, by the minute, or even a split second. The smart passenger plays the brokers against each other and comes out on top. The ship's owner, Mr. Comerford even had a deal of his own. If a passenger was a landowner, and hadn't the fare for passage, he could turn over the deed to his property to Mr. Comerford. To be returned to the rightful owner upon his, or her return to Ireland. After paying the broker, and getting your ticket, it's time for the next step – the medical inspection.

The newly enforced Passenger Act stated that no passenger ship was allowed to leave port until everyone aboard ship had undergone a complete, certified medical inspection. The Medical Inspector, appointed by the Office of Emigration for the Port of Departure, had to inspect the ship's medical chest, to ensure that the proper medications, etc, are sufficient to the number of passengers aboard a ship. The passengers are all checked to make sure they carry no contagious diseases. Whoever charters, is master of, or owns the ship is required to pay 1-pound Sterling for every one hundred passengers inspected, to the Medical Inspector. When a passenger, or a passenger and his family, have all passed the inspection, they have their tickets stamped, and then they are free to do as they please until boarding time. However, any passengers found to be carrying a contagious disease, are not allowed on board. Any family member, or members, if the passengers has family, who are dependent on the discharged person, or are unwilling to leave that person, must depart with him or her. Their personal effects are also taken by that person. All passengers in this situation are entitled to have their fares refunded from the broker, master, or ship's owner by summary process, and by appearing before two or more justices of the peace. After you have successfully undergone the medical inspection, it is on to the next phase.

The next step is the embarkation. It's time to say good-bye loved ones, and old friends. This was both a joyous and tear-filled event.

The scene along the docks of Galway was always a busy one. However, upon the departure of an emigrant ship, with a large complement of passengers on it, the scene became even busier, more exciting, and at times very interesting. Some of the passengers who'd already passed the medical inspection had found berths aboard the ship some twenty-four hours earlier, which was allowed according to English Law.

According to English law, a ship carrying one hundred passengers had to provide a ship's cook, along with a cooking apparatus. Also, a proper amount of fuel for cooking had to be brought on board, space for cooking also had to found; everything being, of course, subject to the approval of the Emigration Officer.

Things are a bit calmer now, as the time for sailing draws near. New arrivals clamber on board and go in search of their own space, in steerage, or in the cabins. Longshoremen are busily tossing luggage from the dock up and onto the ship, where it will be stored at the lowest point in the ship. Latecomers appear, as if to purposefully put off the inevitable until the final seconds. Even though the time of departure has been posted well ahead of time, there are still those who find it desirable to be fashionably late. Finally, it's time to sail. The time of departure is here.

There are always a large number of spectators crowding the docks and quays, to watch the departure of a ship, bound for a foreign land, loaded with its cargo of humanity. Some of the ships are sailing to Australia, Canada, New York, or Philadelphia; the brig *St. John* was destined for Boston. The sight of a great ship being led out of the harbor by a steam tug, can be impressive and awe-inspiring, and even the most indifferent onlooker may well up at the sight, and shed a tear or two. This is the time for the final farewell, the last good-bye, the definitive wave of the hand, for wishing good fortune, and a safe arrival at the next port. As the ship is being towed out to sea; handkerchiefs can be seen fluttering their good-byes. Hats are raised and waved in fond farewells, and from the docks, a loud chorus bids you adieu; and all of the passengers have responded in their own way.

Some tears are shed, and minds fill with fear and regret, at the thought that this may be the last time they will see Ireland: the old country. It's the country they know and love, but it has come to symbolize frustration, pain, and sorrow; starvation and suffering; death and disease. They are saying good-bye to the Ireland of their kin, and their childhood, the land that will stay forever in their hearts, and in their minds.

Sad as this good-bye appears to be, these adventurers know why they are leaving Ireland, why they have chosen to abandon all that they know; and they are looking ahead, to a new way of life, and new opportunities, and a new and different land that lies out there, somewhere, beyond the horizon.

As the tug tows the *St. John* out of Galway Harbor, and into Galway Bay, people are standing in the ship's stern taking their last, long look at Ireland. Others are standing in her bow, looking ahead towards the future. Soon the search for stowaways begins.

The idea of stowing away on board a ship has been practiced for centuries. Stowaways are brought on board hidden in trunks, punctured with air holes to prevent suffocation. Sometimes, they hide in barrels of the ships provisions, buried up to their necks in salt, flour, biscuits, or other such foodstuffs. They hide under bedding, under or in baggage, or in some darkened nook or cranny in the ship's hold, or between decks. It is important to search for these stowaways before the tug has set the ship free, so that if a stowaway is discovered, they can be placed on the tug and returned to port, where they will have to appear before a magistrate.

Although the search for stowaways is done with all due diligence, not every stowaway is caught. In most cases a stowaway may not make an appearance or be caught, for two or three days. By then the ship is too far out to sea to haul back to shore. However, since there is quite a lot to do on a ship at sea, the stowaway, upon discovery, is more often than not, pressed into service. They are forced to work for their passage, and are usually given the most stomach-churning chores to perform – but they do it – or else.

Now that the search for stowaways has been completed, it's time for the captain to call the roll.

Roll call is the final of the six phases the passengers had to endure, and it took the most time. The passengers are ordered to assemble on deck. Those in cabin class did not have to go through this process.

Once thee passengers have gathered, the clerk of the passenger broker, along with the ship's surgeon, aided by the crew, called for the passengers tickets. As each ticket was passed over, the passengers name was written on the ship's register. Once this was completed, they underwent a second medical inspection.

The second medical inspection was done for the benefit of the ship's captain/master, and the ship's owner. The prior inspection was done at the behest of the government. The second one is done for a completely different reason.

When the *St. John* landed in Boston, the ship owner, Henry Comerford, had to pay a tax of $1.50 per passenger. Now, if any of the emigrants were ill in anyway, due to sickness, disease, or deformity, Comerford was fined $75.00 for bringing such a wretch into the Porrt of Boston. The tax was a uniform one. The same in all American ports. Comerford then had to sign a waiver and post a bond, assuring that any person found ill, would not prove to be a public burden. If the Medical Inspector did find anyone who was ill, in one fashion or another and said person cannot prove that he or she has someone to care for them, in Boston for instance, the captain retained the right to keep that person onboard the ship.

Roll call can take up to four hours to be completed satisfactorily, depending upon the number of passengers on a ship, of course, and how many are found to be ill. As the *St. John* pushed its way out of Galway Bay, and past the Aran Islands, roll call was in progress. Luckily, none of her passengers were found to be ill. It would be five long weeks before anyone saw land again.

After a stop in Lettermullen, to pick up another 50-60 passengers, Captain Oliver steers his ship south towards the Canary Islands. After a short stop there its off to the NW and the Gulf Stream, which will take him to America, and Boston.

Therefore, this old and aged ship, her timbers creaking from a human cargo of Irish emigrants, plowed its way westward – Boston was in the distance.

# CHAPTER SEVEN
## THE VOYAGE

And the Voice spoke once again.

"We stood on the docks of Galway, bright, smiling travelers all. Our laughter filled the air; we are joyous, yet nervous. Children scurried about, as mothers gave chase, and once caught both mother and child laughed; it was a fun game they played. Songs are sung; we all joined in. Gulls high above, swooped to and fro, then dove, headlong, into the chilly waters of Galway Bay, for some tasty treat: a fish they'd spied: Lunch! The whole scene was comforting. After all, weren't we sailing into a better life? Weren't the streets of Boston, or for that matter America, paved with gold? Weren't we leaving the death and disease, the pain and the hunger of Ireland for a dream?

"Our home for the next month, at least, would be the brig *St. John*. She was old, and worn with the passage of time. She was rotting, and her timbers and planks groaned out her age. I could see that her rigging had been beaten weary by the winds of years. She couldn't speak her age, but I guessed she was well past thirty; old for a wooden ship. The optimists among us boarded her with nary a care; the pessimists boarded nervously.

"On the morning of September 5, 1849, this old ship unfurled her sails, and with flags a-flying, left the docks of Galway.

"Out, into the harbor, down the bay, past the Twelve Bens and the Aran Islands; into the Atlantic we sailed. We are now eager voyagers, facing west towards an endless horizon, and out there, somewhere: America. All of us, each man, woman, and child looked ahead, to our new lives and new prospects: all of us hoping, planning. We smiled at the thought of friends and family that, within a month, would be greeting us in Boston. There were new homes to build and new ties to be bound. Fortunes would be made; our prospects were fair.

"Westward, ever westward we sailed, to the Land of the Free, and the Home of the Brave. Gone were the dark and gloomy days; that was all behind us now. Ahead, all was sunshine.

"How were we to know the suffering we'd have to endure in the crossing? Forced as we were to live in a hovel, below decks – it is no more than a crowded hell! If we'd only been one of the more fortunate; you know what I mean, don't you? One of those who had that extra pound, that farthing, that pence, to pay for more comfortable lodgings on this hellish ship. We pray and we sing and know that this is only a temporary situation. We know the future is bright. As bright as the sky above, and we sailed on."

Most of the passengers aboard the *St. John* had never been to sea before. The voyagers were, for the most part, farming families. As they inhaled the fetid air of steerage, many began to wretch; this before the Irish coast had faded from view. If things went well and the winds were favorable, the voyage might last five to seven weeks. However, the Atlantic is a fickle ocean, and her gales, headwinds, and mountainous swells turned many a crossing into a ten to twelve week nightmare. Add to this the threat of disease and you have a ship full of terrified, sick, yet hopeful passengers.

Imagine a ship that is loaded with passengers, both the healthy and the sick, in overcrowded quarters, packed in as a human ballast, as tight as sardines, in the deepest reaches of this ship; a ship built not for this cargo of humanity, but for goods, to be transported across this long and barren seascape. They were huddled en masse, without light, or fresh air, living in filth and breathing the disease carrying, dead air of steerage. These pilgrims are dead! Dead in mind! Dead in spirit! Dead in soul! Dead in faith! Yet, they are willing to bear the insufferable for the chance that America brings to them.

Tears were shed openly, and sobs heard as the ship pushed its way into the open sea.

Now these Pilgrims are no more than a huddled mass of humanity, living or dying at the whim of a dangerous, unforgiving landscape none are familiar with. They hold tight to each other, their rosaries, and they pray as one. Some gasp, others scream, as the great ship is played by the oceans swells and the tender ship rises and falls like a cork. All the passengers could do was hope that this ship made it safely to Boston.

Soon enough some made the adjustment to life at sea, and the oceans rhythm. Most days were sun-filled, with clear blue skies overhead, and a brisk breeze that carried them easily over the ocean. They talked of the future in the soft Gaelic tongues, so familiar to them. They watched as the sails unfurled and went full, capturing the new days breeze, and they smiled in the realization that the wind was carrying them closer to Boston and a new and better way of life.

Soon, perhaps, a fiddler would have everyone, especially the children, stepping to some frolicsome tune, or singing with him the songs, some plaintive, others merry, of their native Ireland.

Hearts beat wildly as September sailed into October. "It can't be far away now," one might have said. They had been at sea for almost a month; America was out there, some- where, close. Everyday now, they stood on the deck, by the ship's rail, straining for even a glimpse of the Land of Milk and Honey.

When on October 6, 1849, they first glimpsed the coast of America, many counted the hours until they'd see old friends and family, waiting for them on the docks of Boston.

# CHAPTER EIGHT
## CAPE COD

Thoreau wrote of Cape Cod in his book of the same title, describing the Cape thusly: and I quote. "Cape Cod is the bared and bended arm of Massachusetts; the shoulder at Buzzard's Bay; the elbow, or crazy bone at Cape Mallebarre; the wrist at Truro; and the sandy fist at Provincetown, - behind which the state stands on her guard, with her back at the Green Mountains, and her feet planted on the floor of the ocean, like an athlete protecting the bay, - boxing with northeast storms, and ever anon, heaving up her Atlantic adversary from the lap of the earth, - ready to thrust forward her other fist, which keeps guard the while upon her breast at Cape Ann."

The voyage across the Atlantic was a pleasant one: smooth and uneventful, and five weeks out of Galway, Captain Oliver spotted the cliffs of North Truro, and Cape Cod Light.

Cape Cod, or Highland Light, as it is also known, was erected in 1797, at the request of President George Washington. In 1776, two acres of land on the eastern side of Cape Cod, in North Truro, in Barnstable County, were purchased from Isaac Small of Truro, for $110. Since there had been more shipwrecks here than on any other part of cape Cod, due for the most part to the nefarious Peaked Hill Bars, it was decided by the federal government to build a lighthouse on this point of land.

The original tower, built in 1797, was situated on what is known as the Clay Pounds, a cliff 183 feet above the shore; the light was built 500 feet from the edge of Truro Cliff. Today that distance is 125 feet from the cliff, as a result of the erosion of the cliff (in 1996, the lighthouse was moved back to protect it from the continually eroding cliff).

The 45-foot wooden structure that became the lighthouse was, the first lighthouse on Cape Cod, the first flashing light, the sixth lighthouse erected by the federal government, the ninth lighthouse along the coast of Massachusetts, and the twenty-first lighthouse built in America. The light, which could be seen, on a clear night 18 miles out to sea, was lit by 24 whale oil lamps. In 1831, a new tower, made of New Hampshire granite, was erected. Cape Cod Light is usually the first light seen by ships entering Massachusetts Bay, from Europe.

The Peaked Hill Bars are found three miles NE of Cape Cod Light. It was on these bars, on November 2, 1778, that *H.M.S. Somerset* ran aground and wrecked. The *Somerset* was the same ship that Paul Revere had been rowed past, with muffled oars, in the waters off Charlestown, prior to setting out on his "Midnight Ride." The *Somerset* also played a major role in the Battle of Bunker Hill, when parts of her crew rowed British reinforcements across the Mystic, to take part in the third and final assault on the hill.

On November 2, 1778, the *Somerset* was caught in a gale as she attempted to make Provincetown Harbor. The ship's captain, George Owry, struggled to keep the great ship on course. He soon found himself wallowing in the dangerous waters known as "The Triangle," where Pollock Rip Shoals, the Chatham Shoals, and the Truro Highlands, all come together. Soon enough, the Peaked hill Bars reached out and grabbed the foundering old warrior. Try as he might, Owry could not save his ship, and the Bars slowly sucked the ship in. Finally, with a lurch and a great bump. the great ship's keel stuck in the sand of the Outer Bar; the *Somerset* would sail no more. Days later her 34-cannon were removed and hauled to Boston. The irony that lovers of history enjoy showed itself yet again,. On April 7, 1779, almost four years to the day that he'd slipped silently past the sleeping *Somerset* in the waters off Charlestown, Colonel Paul Revere place twenty of the *Somerset's* cannons on platforms at Castle Island, in Boston Harbor.

Cape Cod Light had been sighted at 5 p.m., October 6. Captain Oliver then called all of the passengers up on deck, telling them, happily, "The end of your journey is near, as we are but one day out of Boston. Tonight shall be your last night upon the *St. John*," and he smiled, as cheers filled the air.

Next, Oliver places the names of 100 passengers on the ships manifest, as he calls the roll. He then draws a line on the deck, and the passengers behind that line have their names entered into a second, or alternate book – why is this done? Finally, after all the names had been entered into one of the two books, Captain Oliver calls for a celebration.

The passengers and crew happy that the journey was near its end, prepared an illumination, and the deck and rigging were soon decorated with candles. Captain Oliver passed out "a measure of ardent spirit," and most of the passengers and crew partook of the treat. The rest of the evening was spent in song, dance, and celebration; the passengers had ample reason for celebration. Behind then they'd left the death, disease, and hunger of Ireland. Ahead of them lay the Land of Opportunity. As they rounded the tip of Cape Cod, at Provincetown, the weather began to thicken, and a light breeze began to blow. Oliver hove his ship to and set a NE heading.

In Concord, author and Transcendentalist Henry David Thoreau, and his friend, poet Ellery Channing, had just finalized their plans for a trip to Cape Cod. In Cohasset, young Elizabeth Lothrop finished the latest entry into her diary, and then fell asleep. Captain Daniel Lothrop may have been sitting by the fire, reading, as its glow warmed him; his brother John Jacob Lothrop, may have just fallen into a deep sleep. Doctor Fordyce Foster, the town physician, had been busy all day long visiting patients and may have just finished a late meal. Down at the harbor, Michael Neptune Brennock was standing at the harbor's edge, studying the waves as they crashed up against Tower's Wharf, located across from his house. The Gove Family was fast asleep. Charles Studley had just visited Whitehead to check on the condition of the town's two lifeboats, located there. After bailing one out, he returned home. On the Common, across from the First Paris Church, the Reverend Joseph Osgood had just finished writing the next day's sermon. James St. John and his family slept soundly.

Off shore, the spider-like edifice that would become the First Minot's Light, quivered nervously in the strengthening winds. In three months it would be lit for the first time.

By one o'clock on the morning of October 7th, the winds had changed and started howling NNE: three hours later, they changed to ENE.

In Boston, anxious families waited nervously, yet eagerly, for word that the *St. John* had arrived safely. Mr. Eliot, the British Consul, was fast asleep after a long day of meetings. The husband of Peggy Adams, and her sister, both of South Boston, waited with hearts-a-flutter, for Peggy' long awaited arrival. Patrick Kennelly had a fitful sleep, he could hardly wait to see his wife Bridget, and their three children, after so long a separation. Mrs. Mulkenan, of 4th Street, South Boston, smiled before dousing her candle. Soon she'd be reunited with her three daughters Honora, Mary, and Margaret. In Lynn, Honora Donnelly's sister waited patiently. Honora Donnelly was sixteen years old. Out in the western part of the state, in Springfield, Massachusetts, a Mrs. McDermott waited for the arrival of her two sisters.

# CHAPTER NINE
## BOSTON

Now that they were less than a day away from Boston. let's look at what awaited these Irish Immigrants. The Boston these Irish folk were coming to at this time was not about to open its arms and welcome them happily. The city had, in 1849, a population of about 110,000 people, most of whom could trace their ancestry back to the *Mayflower*. Boston was a Puritan, Anglo-Saxon, and Protestant community, filled with many prejudices. The prominent names in the city were Cabot, Lowell, Saltonstall, Peabody, and Weld; they were the "Boston Brahmin." Bostonians were more than willing to send food or money to help the famine-ridden Irish; as long as they stayed in Ireland. There was no room for such people in Boston. As they started arriving by the boatload, "Proper Bostonians," did their nest to keep them down; the Protestant-Irish did have a bit easier, but not much.

In 1820, there were 2,000 Irish living in Boston. By 1825, there were 5,000, and by 1830, 7,000 sons and daughters of Erin, called Boston home. In 1847, alone, 13,235 Irish immigrants arrived in Boston and its environs. By 1850, Boston had the highest concentration of Irish in the United States.

The newly arriving Irish had one built-in strike against them – Catholicism. So great was their distrust of anything Catholic, that Protestant Boston immediately ostracized them. It would get so bad, that a mob of Protestant workers put the torch to a Catholic convent, in Roxbury.

It was said that the Irish were an angry, sullen, and alcoholic people, reveling and debauching into the wee hours of the morning. Bostonians saw the Irish as clannish, greedy, illiterate people, who fornicated like bunnies. Insanity and prostitution plagued them.

They were laughed at and openly ridiculed by the "proper citizens" of Boston; Irishmen were arrested for public drunkenness more often; their children ran wild in the streets. It was this hatred, this lack of social acceptance, which drove the Irish in on themselves, and the Catholic Church. This gave rise, albeit slowly, to the founding of financial institutions designed to help only the Irish.

For the most part, the Irish enclave was centered in Boston's North End, not far from the birthplaces of Benjamin Franklin and Paul Revere, and the sights of the Boston Tea Party, the Boston Massacre, and the Old North Church. Soon, the Irish would make up over half of the North End's population. At the time of the *St. John's* sailing some of Boston's Irish were also living in Dorchester and South Boston.

Part of the reason that many Irish had come to America, was to escape their unscrupulous landlairds; they were forced to live in hovels, to work barely arable lands, and to pay exhorbitant rents. Sadly, the Irish ran into more of the same, if not worse, in Boston.

They were packed, sardine-like into decrepit one-bedroom apartments, or ramshackle boarding houses. Once beautiful, and spacious homes, were hollowed out, and transformed into cheap apartment houses, with the landlord charging up to $1.50 per week for a 9x12, casket of a room, with no water, no sanitation, no ventilation, and no light. The proper authorities did nothing to enforce the city's sanitary codes: building codes were non-existent. There were no safety codes to speak of, so the landlords could do as they pleased, without fear of reprisal.

A single-family, three-story dwelling on Boston Harbor could easily be cut up into housing for one hundred or more Irish immigrants, giving its owner a substantial profit. All along the waterfront, old warehouses and other abandoned buildings were converted into housing for the newly arriving Irish. The rooming houses barely provided shelter, and the walls were so thin that you had no privacy at all. Yet there was an overflow, so great was the demand for housing. This overflow lived where they could; in musty old cellars with low ceilings, which would flood at high tide; in wooden shacks, gardens, and alleyways: even in back yards. It was an ugly, squalid existence. There were no comforts, no necessities, huddled together as they were, without regard to age, sex, or sense of decency. Such an existence causes the loss of one's self respect and virtue, which are replaced by desperation, disarray, and indifference. Drunkenness and boredom reigned supreme: the Irish were desperate. The crime rate rose to ridiculous levels, as the Irish clung desperately to the edge of the American abyss.

Conditions such as these became the Irish Petrie Dish for diseases such as cholera. In Boston's Irish community, the disease and mortality rates became the highest in the city; so was its literacy rate. Boston doctors would later say, "Irish children are born to die." Sixty percent of all Irish children would die before reaching the age of six; many an Irish adult, be they male or female lived the same number of years after arriving in Boston.

The Irish, unlike earlier waves of immigrants: Italians, Jews, or the Portuguese, had few resources, or skills, to aid in their adjustment. Opportunities for employment were few. As anti-Irish sentiments grew, "N.I.N.A.'s: *"No Irish Need Apply"* signs could be seen throughout the city. As such, the Irish were resigned to; more like forced to, take any job available, usually the lowest and most menial job. Their women became domesTics. Their working conditions were safe, but at times inhumane. Irish men became canal diggers and day laborers, doing such things as filling in Boston's Back bay, building bridges, roadways, and building what would later become Boston's Transit System. Many took factory jobs, inside and outside the city.

Even as much as two years after the wreck of the *St. John*, this unforgiving attitude remained. An Unknown writer wrote these next few words, giving hope to the Irish, and I quote. "People accuse the Irish of being an idle and shiftless people. They have no motive to work. The Irish laborer has not had a fair chance. Give him his rights, and then see if his arms are not as strong, and his will as hearty, as that of the free and independent laborer of America."

This was the new world, the world of hope, of opportunity, that the passengers on the *St. John* were sailing into.

# CHAPTER TEN
## SCITUATE

For eight hours the *St. John* did battle with what had become, by this time, a full-blown nor'easter. By 1 a.m., October 7, she had managed to make Scituate Light, at Cedar Point.

Scituate Light is located at the mouth of Scituate Harbor, on Cedar Point. She is made of Quincy granite, and stands 50' tall. The lighthouse was erected in 1811. Skippers often confused Boston Light with Scituate Light, and the result was a continual litany of ship-wrecks. Schooners, barques, brigs, and numerous other types of ships, crashed with disheartening regularity on the dangerous and deadly Cohasset Rocks, located in the passageway into Boston Harbor. During the War of 1812, a British warship dropped anchor and lolled lazily in the waters off Cedar Point, with plans to enter the harbor and attack the town. Across the harbor, in their fathers home, the Bates sisters, Abigail and Rebecca, spotted the ship, and seeing the situation might be desperate, acted quickly and efficiently. Grabbing their fife and drum, the sisters marched towards the lighthouse. They caused such a ruckus that the British captain thought the town militia had been called out, en masse, to defend the town. The ship's anchor was hauled up, and she floated safely away, unscathed. This is how Scituate's "Army of Two" defeated the British without firing a shot.

Captain Oliver worked feverishly to keep the *St. John* on an ENE heading. He steered the ship slowly against a harsh and adverse wind, until he had reached an area somewhere outside Boston harbor. Standing off, the wind suddenly changed, and began blowing violently from the NE, halting any further headway. Now Oliver made the first of many fatal decisions; he ordered the ship turned around, heading her back into the deeper, safer waters of Massachusetts Bay; he hoped to ride out the storm, and sail the *St. John* safely into port after the storm abated. Unfortunately, he was unable to stabilize the ship, and she drifted with the winds. The winds were so vicious by now that the ship was being forced WSW, closer and closer to shore; the *St. John* was entangled in the worst storm of the season. Past Quincy, Weymouth, Hingham, and Hull, and she continued to be carried away by the winds. Oliver stood the ship to the north, hoping to avoid the coast, but all to no avail. By 4 a.m., the *St. John* was nearing Outer Minot Ledge, and the murderous Cohasset Rocks. Here he stood the ship to the SW.

The watches on deck may have sought shelter by this time. The storm was raging now. Anxious passengers below deck tried to encourage each other; there was still hope. The storm may dampen the body, but not the spirit.

On deck, things were frightful, and less than encouraging. The wind was whipping in a frenzy, giant whitecaps were seen everywhere; it was a desperate situation. Dawn broke as the *St. John* pitched and rolled on an angry sea. For two more hours, Oliver tacked the ship; the weather was frightful by this time. By 6 a.m., the *St. John* was inside of Inner Minot Ledge. Those on deck watched in silence, as storm-driven was crashed into and over the granite monster that was the ledge.

# CHAPTER ELEVEN
## COHASSET

The name Cohasset means, "The long, rocky, place," how appropriate. This is an Anglicized version of its Indian name, Quonihassit, and the name of the Native American tribe that inhabited this area long ago. Captain John Smith explored these waters before the Pilgrims landed in Plymouth; he was in Cohasset in 1614.

Cohasset men have fought in King Phillip's War, the French-Indian War, the Revolution, the War of 1812, the Mexican War, the Civil War, the Spanish-American War, World War One, World War Two, Korea, Vietnam, the Gulf War, in Iraq, and Afghanistan.

Much like Boston, and most of America at the time, Cohasset was a Puritan, Protestant-English town. The ruling tribes, so to speak, were named Bates, Lothrop, Tower, Pratt, and Stoddard. Located in Norfolk County, Cohasset is bordered by Scituate, Hingham, Hull, and Norwell, with the Atlantic Ocean as its angry neighbor to the east. Although Cohasset is a rough and rocky place, farming as well as the sea, was a major industry in town. Cushing farm was located near the center of the village. The Doane Farm, found on Jerusalem Road, is still active under the name Holly Hill farm. There were numerous farms on the Lincoln Hillside, the most noted being the Oaks farm. In Beechwood, most of that area was taken up by smaller farms and mills.

Cohasset, in 1849, was better known as a seafaring community. Up to ten, if not more, wharves ringed Cohasset harbor. Many of the men were fishermen, or lobstermen, doing their life's work off the coast, and dancing, carefully, with the Cohasset Rocks. Besides fishing, Cohasset men built and skippered numerous deep-sea trading and fishing vessels.

By the 1840's, the Cohasset mackerel fleet numbered fifty schooners, alone. The list of sea captains that sailed out of Cohasset, or its environs, reached well past thirty. Captain James Collier probably captained more ships and logged more sea miles, than any seafaring man of his era (1813-1891).

In the village, you had the Unitarian Church (The 1st Parish Church), the 1st Congregaional Church (The 2nd Parish Church), which was located across the street from the Unitarian by the Common; there was no Catholic Church in town at this time.

The *St. John* pitched and rolled, she moaned and groaned, up and down she went, as the waves toyed with her, and the winds took her where *they* wanted. She was struggling to maintain her composure, to get back on a straight course. Hearts grew weaker with each passing minute, heads dipped, and then sunk into chests, as death stared these immigrants in the eye and winked.

Cries are heard and screams echoed throughout the ship. Mothers held their children tightly, husbands embraced and held tight their wives and children, one final time; friends bade each other a fond farewell, or good luck. It was dark down below, and felt even more cramped as bodies were being tossed angrily, to and fro, by each successive wave that beat into the foundering ship. Off in the distance Outer Minot Ledge beckoned, and a mile inside of that, the "Sleeping Whales waited: Grampus Ledge was ready to claim another victim.

# CHAPTER TWELVE
## GRAMPUS LEDGE

Grampus Ledge
A Hynaku
By Tirell
(Found at allpoetry.com)

Teeth
Shrouded mists
Await natures ideal.


And the voice continued.
"We were farmers for the most part, and a month at sea seemed such a long time. Thankfully, the voyage was uneventful. Then, from the northeast came a tempest, as if tossed upon us by the Almighty himself. The weak, old ship moaned. Her timbers and planks cried and twisted in pain. Her sails were torn asunder: nothing but tattered ribbons now. The wind screamed and howled in anger, its teeth bared. The ship is off course now, adrift in an angry, unforgiving landscape that none of us is familiar with; there's no place to hide, nowhere for us to find shelter from this storm. We are at the mercy of this wind, this sea; we are but the helpless sport of waters.

"We're in the breakers now; Oh God, save us! Show us your merciful hand! I cried out. Then, we strike Grampus Ledge, and hold fast. Now the ship is beaten, and pounded, and she broke. Her seams split, her spine is severed, and she died, a paralyzed hulk. We are all cast to the seas," and here the voice paused.

"Survivors have spoken and historians have written of the wreck of the St. John. Much of what has been written is fact: some is fiction. Writers have tried, in vain, to describe the pain we endured, our frantic efforts to retain life, of the wild thoughts that ran through our minds, as we prepared to meet our maker. Only a survivor can accurately tell those stories, or describe those feelings; only a survivor can fully describe what it is like to reach shore after fighting through the raging gale and those angry seas. How can you describe hearing the screams of men, women, and children: your husband, your wife, or your child? How can you make someone understand what it is like to watch a boat, filled with people, capsize, or break apart, and watch those people struggling, vanish beneath the waves? Only a survivor can do that. Only a survivor can describe the feelings, the thoughts that drift through the mind as you cling to a piece of that destroyed boat as it carries them towards shore. Only a survivor can tell you what it feels like to be beaten on a rock by angry waves; what it feels like to touch the shore, only to be carried away, back into the sea by the tide or a wave; only a survivor can tell you, honestly, about the wreck of the St. John.

"Cruelly, tragically, ironically, our trip was over. Perhaps Fate played a part in it all. We'd left the death, disease and tragedy of Ireland, only to meet Death off Cohasset. We could see America within our grasp. So happy we were, so hopeful we felt. Now, there are few of us left. Twenty-two of us reached a safe harbor."

A grampus is a member of the animal kingdom. A Chordata of the family Delphinidae, of the Cetacea order; a mammal. The genus is Orcinus, the species, Orcinus Orca. A killer whale, also known as Blackfish, Grampus, and Orca, and because males are known to have a tall dorsal fin, aka: Swordfish. Other names have been used such as, Grampus Orca, and Orca Gladiator. Such whales are known as Grampus Griesus, and are related to and resemble dolphins, but lack the beak-like snout of the dolphin.

Grampus Ledge can be found between the Western Channel and the Gangway, outside of Cohasset Harbor. It is considered a bar, by some. The depth of the waters at this ledge, or bar, is 20', maximum. It is located at 42-15-57N and 70-46-48W.

As the black of night dissipated into the grey of an angry dawn, Oliver spotted another ship inside Minot's Ledge: she was the British brig, Kathleen. Oliver decided to make a run for the harbor, in hopes of wearing up to the Kathleen. With the storm's rage ever increasing, and the waves mounting ever higher, he made his run. He ordered the sails reefed, but the winds threaten to pull the great masts right out of the ship, so he stayed the order. Unfortunately, Oliver couldn't close on the Kathleen: so high were the winds, and so rough was the sea. By now, her masts had been torn to shreds. The storm, it seemed was too powerful to fight. In an effort to steady his ship, Capt. Oliver dropped both his anchors, and with a rattle of chains they went out, finally touching bottom. With a great shudder, the ship came to a stop, and held its place. However, the anchors couldn't hold her; they were unable to handle the forces of nature, and they began to drag, as each successive wave carried her closer to the Grampus. Oliver then ordered all his masts cut away, and they fell into the sea with a barely discernible splash, which steadied the floundering ship momentarily. However, the jettisoning of masts, rigging, and the dropping of anchors, did nothing to stop the inevitable; the Grampus was closing in. Now the wind cried out in anger, nature was seeking her revenge, and the St. John continued to drag her anchors, pushing her ever closer to her doom. On shore, those watching from Cohasset or Scituate, said a prayer, aloud or to themselves, praying that the ship could somehow escape the Grampus, and the other Cohasset Rocks. However, the seas were mountainous, the winds relentless, as the ship was pushed even closer to its inevitable demise. Below decks, Acts of Contrition were being said in agonized Gaelic. Then, sometime between seven and seven-thirty on the morning of October 7, 1849, the St. John collided with Grampus Ledge.

Up in Boston, word of the perils of the St. John and the Kathleen had been received. The steamer, R.B. Forbes was made ready, and then sent out to aid in the rescue of those aboard both troubled ships. No sooner had the steamer reached the waters of Massachusetts Bay, than she was forced to turn about, and head back in to Boston Harbor; she had split her mainsail, and would be of no use in the perilous waters off Cohasset. Ironically, two years later the Forbes would be stationed off Minot Ledge, as the first of three lightships used there after the collapse of the first Minot Light.

The people of Cohasset had awoken to the first nor'easter of the season, and were soon made aware of the two ships in danger off their coast. A crowd of locals had gathered on both the Cohasset and Scituate shores, and they looked out in awe, as events unfolded before misty eyes.

At eight o'clock that morning, 19 year-old Elizabeth Lothrop's attention was drawn to the waters outside of her house; her brothers had spotted the Kathleen and the St. John, in trouble among the rocks. One ship appeared to be a safe distance from the nasty Cohasset Rocks that line this part of the Massachusetts coastline (this was the Kathleen). The St. John was in grave danger, as it was being forced closer to Grampus Ledge. Elizabeth immediately informed her father of the situation. He set out, immediately, for the town's two lifeboats, located nearby at Whitehead.

As she watched in horror from her home, and her brothers watched from the beach at Sandy Cove, the St. John began to drift. She prayed the ship's anchors would hold, if they didn't the ship would soon be dashed onto Grampus Ledge. She watched wide-eyed and awed, as the ship was forced upon that ledge; an hour later, the ship was gone.

The scene as witnessed from the shore had to have been both heartbreaking, as well as horrifying. No sooner had the St. John struck the Grampus, when a huge mountain of a wave; some witnesses would say it was well over 50' high, washed completely over the desperate ship, carrying to their watery-deaths, dozens upon dozens of poor, unsuspecting Irish immigrants, crowded on her decks. Another wave followed and swept that deck clear of any remnant of humanity; it was this second wave that swept Patrick Sweeney's wife and 10 children into the sea.

Now the ocean is covered with the dead, dying, and those that might survive. Those still alive in that sea are desperate, frantic, and screaming for help: there will be no help. Those on-shore, swore they could hear

## On Grampus Ledge

the pitiful cries and screams of the dying, as they were propelled into an angry sea. Within minutes, the brig St. John was no more.

There was no ship left, to speak of, and few if any passengers could have survived such an event. As of yet no attempt had been made to launch the lifeboat, in hopes that both ships could escape their situations unscathed: but that all changed. By 8:00 a.m., the Cohasset lifeboat had been pulled into the pounding surf. She was successfully launched after several failed attempts.

Those on shore waved hats or yelled for they could see people gathered on what remained of the struggling ship's deck. In reality, what they were attempting to do was to get the attention of the lifeboat crew, praying that they could get to the beleaguered ship before it was much too late. However, those in the lifeboat never saw those frantic signals, nor those clinging desperately to the shattered remnants of the St. John.

Yet another monstrous wave was making its silent yet deadly approach, and when it hit the ship, it dashed her hard upon Grampus Ledge. She teetered there momentarily, as the wind tortured her, and the waves, never-ending, pounded her mercilessly upon that craggy ledge. Up she went, only to be dropped violently; and the helpless ship took her beating. Soon her seams popped and her back broke. Between the granite-ledged Grampus, and the relentless pounding of the surf, in combination with a howling nor-easter, the ships hull gave way; a gaping hole was now torn into her side. Wave after wave rushed in to claim their victims. In seconds, everyone below decks was dead, adrift in a rubbish-laden sea, among the bodies of their friends and families, and the remnants of their lives. Within the hour, parts of her hull would be found on shore. It is doubtful that even a ship of steel could have survived the beating the St. John took.

The sea poured into that gaping hole, engulfing and drowning the passengers still trapped below decks. And the sea continued its pounding. By 8 a.m., and hour or so after she'd struck, the St. John had gone completely to pieces.

In the midst of all the violence, and before she'd broken up, the ship's jollyboat was made ready, Unfortunately, she'd been hanging by her tackle alongside the ship, when her stern bolt snapped, depositing her into the sea, landing bottom up. Capt. Oliver, his 2nd mate, and

Paul A. Fiori

four of the crew plunged into the water, righted the boat, and managed to climb into the jolly. Then, twenty-five passengers tried to save their own lives by climbing into the small vessel; this decision swamped the jolly, sinking it. The 2nd mate, two of the crew, and twenty-five passengers perished. One passenger and Captain Oliver were pulled to safety by Henry Comerford, the 1st mate, and the nephew of the ship's owner.

The Cohasset Lifeboat was pounding its way through the angry seas. Over on the Grampus, the St. John was no more, and the waters nearby were covered with pieces of the wreck; to which many of the passengers were clinging desperately, as wave after wave broke over them.

The St. John's longboat had broken loose, but Capt. Oliver, Henry Comerford, seven more of the crew, and two passengers, managed to board her safely. At this point, it is alleged that Oliver gave orders that no effort was to be made to pick up survivors.

As the men rowed their way towards the Glades one of the ship's passengers, Patrick Sweeney, swimming desperately and clutching his infant daughter, almost made it safely to the longboat, but as those in the lifeboat watched helplessly, Sweeney and his daughter, slipped silently beneath the waves. Patrick Sweeney, his wife, and eleven children, all drowned that morning. Thirty other passengers also drowned, attempting to reach the longboat.

After forty-five minutes of backbreaking effort, the lifeboat crew spotted the longboat, making its way to the safe shore of the Glades. No one will ever know if the men in those two boats ever spoke with each other. What is a fact is that the Cohasset Lifeboat rowed over to the Kathleen, and rescued her crew. Maybe the lifesavers assumed that all in the longboat were all that remained of the passengers and crew of the St. John: maybe that is what Captain Oliver told them! In reality, the lifesavers never spotted the St. John, due to the height of the waves that morning, and knew nothing of her perils.

By nine o'clock that morning, Captain Oliver, and those in the longboat, had made it safely to the Glades. Saved were Captain Oliver, Henry and Isaac Comerford, Henry O'Hearn, Michael Kennelly, William Larkin, Thomas Walker, James Flaherty, Andrew Frost, and two unnamed passengers.

At the Lothrop House, Elizabeth was preparing the house for any survivors that might be brought there; this house being the closest to the scene of the on-going tragedy. Fireplaces were lit, bed linen was changed, water was heated, and she simmered a bottle of wine.

The ship was gone, Oliver and those in the longboat were on their way to the Glades, and the lifeboat was on the way over to the Kathleen. Debris as well as dead bodies floated silently to shore, yet, on shattered pieces of the St. John's hull clung seven women and three men. These pieces of the once great ship were now serving as rafts, and they drifted anxiously towards shore, saving their ten passengers. By this time, the waters off Cohasset were a mess of wreckage, baggage, and dead, dying, and living bodies. Those that made it to shore alive, or dead, washed up at Sandy Cove, Bigelow's Beach, Quarry Point, or Whitehead, about ½ a mile from Sandy Cove. On one piece of wreckage that washed ashore there were two dead bodies clinging to it, both were badly beaten.

Down at the beach, those residents trying to pull the survivors to safety were having a difficult time. The rough surf would dash those clinging to life on the wreckage, upon the rocks that surrounded the beach, and then draw them slowly back into the sea. Clinging with a death-like grip to their piece of wreckage some made it to shore. When they reached land, they hung on desperately to the legs or clothing of their saviors; some were seen muttering a silent prayer to their savior. One of those saved, a woman, had been badly beaten upon the rocks, but in spite of the beating, she managed a hurt smile. It was felt that she would not survive the evening. However, by the following morning, she was in a much better way and she would live.

Two other women had also taken a beating, and may not live the night. One of them had severe bruising about her head from the rocks and wreckage that assaulted her on the way in. The other woman, who may have a husband living in Boston, lost her three children in the disaster (This was either Honora Burke or Honora Cullen).

The survivors were beaten, bruised, and cold. In some cases, they were out of their minds. The town's doctor, Dr. Fordyce Foster, did his best attending to their needs, and all appeared to be recovering as well as could be expected. One of those rescued, a Mrs. Quinlan, had taken a harsher beating than many. She had suffered head wounds, and both internal and external injuries. She was expected to live, however.

Dr. Foster lived at 55 North Main Street, near the church. Dr. Foster was married to Adeline Tower of Cohasset. The Fosters had six children: Ellen, Julia, Nichols, Elizabeth, Addie, and Harriet. In later years, he was also a selectman.

Honora Burke was in a tougher and much more difficult position. Due to the severity of her injuries, she fluctuated between life and death. However, she was holding her own, and, it was soon discovered, she was pregnant. Dr. Foster felt that both she and the baby would be just fine given rest.

The survivors were soon brought to the Lothrop house. Glancing out the window, Elizabeth Lothrop spotted what she would later describe in her diary as "…miserable looking creatures," the first of the victims to make it to the house; they reminded her of nothing more than drowned rats! They had difficulty walking, and were being guided by their saviors, who were supporting them as they trudged slowly, yet heavily, along. Soon the door to the house opened and they were welcomed by Miss Lothrop.

The first to be brought in were two men, and a while later came the women. Fear was etched upon the faces, as they sat by the fires glow, shivering and sipping the warmed wine. Soon they were placed in beds, or on couches, and all effort was made to restore their beaten and bruised bodies, and souls. All day and into the early evening the moans and cries of the battered Irish pilgrims echoed throughout the house. Two of the women seemed to have lost their minds, as they babbled on, incoherently. By nightfall, six of these wretches would be taken to the Alm's House. Finally, Elizabeth Lothrop had a moment to rest. However, the sight of that ship being beaten on that ledge, and the sad condition of the survivors, would stay with her forever.

In all twelve passengers (other reports say ten) clinging to anything that floated, or washing in on a wave, managed to survive. They were: Austin Kearin (20), Betsey Higgins (21), Michael Fitzpatrick (26), Barbara Kennelly (20), Michael Redding (24), Mary Honora Burke (27, who lost three children), Catherine Flanagan (20), Mary Kane (24), Michael Gibbon (26), Mary Slattery (20), a Mrs. Quinlan, and Honora Cullen (who lost three children). Some of those who survived had to have their hands pried from their life-saving wreckage. One of those who survived was a 14-year-old stowaway; he may have been one of the two passengers that were in Capt. Oliver's longboat. He had hidden himself on board because his sisters were headed to Boston, on board the ill-fated St. John. When the ship struck Grampus Ledge, he jumped into the jollyboat, which swamped. Swimming to safety, and later pulled from the sea by 1st mate Henry Comerford, he found himself in the longboat, thus his life was saved. His sisters had drowned. Six of the survivors were taken to the home of John Jacob Lothrop. The Lothrop home on Atlantic Avenue had been opened in 1740 as a seaside inn and tavern, named The Whittington Hotel. By 1785, it was a private home. The current address is 159 Atlantic Avenue. Six others were taken to the home of Captain Abraham Tower, near the Common.

Lothrop, it seems, was involved in a strange, yet wonderful experience, amid all the horror that day. As he stood on the shore with the waves breaking all around him, he watched a small package of what he thought were goods, riding high upon the crest of a wave. Watching carefully, he times the rhythm of the waves; he hoped to save even this small package. As he watched and waited, the package came near, and then it hit him square in the face, when the wave carrying it, came crashing to shore. Grabbing at the package before it drifted away, he pulled it closer to him. Holding it in his hands now, he opened it, and he soon beheld the sight of a live infant. The mother had wrapped her child in the blanket, and committed her child's body to the sea, praying that God might save her child's life. The child was safe and alive now. But things might not have been so if not for a mother's love, a strangers care, and the loving hand of God. Taking the child in his arms, Lothrop brought it his home and later gave the child to the Gove family.

The Gove family lived on Border Street, down along the harbor. Mr. Gove was a painter and paperhanger. He and his wife Eliza had six children. Two daughters, Josephine (1835-1836) and Elizabeth (1839-1839), lived less than a year each. The other four children, Otis, Harriot, William, and Alonzo, lived fine lives.

Another source states that the child was later taken in by a Norwell family. She grew up and married a Boston man who became wealthy in the land business. Whether or not this is true has never been definitively proven.

# CHAPTER THIRTEEN
## OCTOBER 8
## THE SEARCH

A weakened and sad voice recalls the events of that dreadful day.

"Sandy Cove, Cohasset, the day after the storm, lay strewn with the debris of the ship, her passengers and crew. The waves would roll in, recede, and in their wake, deposit more wreckage. Bodies lay still, dead, as the sea, that once angry, yet still turbulent foe, kissed and caressed each of the deceased, before departing, as if to say I win! Or fare thee well!

"The loved ones of us, the dearly departed, have arrived. They are desperate; a more somber, sadder group cannot be found this day. The search is on for friends or family, hoping, even in death, that they, the living can recover what they cherish most. Many, sadly, found no body or bodies to claim.

"A mother, perhaps from Boston, has come in search of her baby. The child was coming to Boston with her aunt. The bodies were found: the aunt holding the baby close to her breast. The mother, the sister, wailed, moaned, and then collapsed: she died three days later. This wreck had claimed another victim."

At daybreak, the scene on the beach and for a mile or so further, was both devastating and enervating to the living. The coast for that mile or so was covered with the flotsam and jetsam of the passengers and crew of the St. John, and of the ship itself. Over the course of the night, twenty more bodies washed ashore and had been recovered; most of the dead had been horribly mutilated. One woman's forehead had been shorn of its skin right down to her skull. Another victim had the flesh torn from his right leg, from the knee to his foot. Other bodies were in a similar, if not worse state of being. As the day wore on, three of the bodies were positively identified: they were the nieces of the ship's owner, Henry Comerford.

By this time, word of the disaster had spread past the borders of Cohasset, up to Boston, the towns in between, and south of Cohasset. Scituate residents were well aware of what had happened, since some of them had watched the drama unfold from the Glades, and due to the fact that Capt. Oliver had saved himself, and others at the Glades in Scituate. By noon, Oliver and those in the longboat were back in Cohasset.

Soon, this small seacoast community, no more than a dot on any map, was filled with the curious. Up in Boston, a handbill had been printed, stating: "Death! 145 lives lost off Cohasset!" Two interested readers of that handbill were, author Henry David Thoreau, and his friend, poet Ellery Channing. Deciding that the sight of a shipwreck might be an interesting experience, Thoreau convinced Channing to make the trip; plus it would give Thoreau a chance to see his old friends the Reverend Joseph Osgood and his wife, Ellen.

By noon, the shoreline was packed with people active in the recovery process. As these would-be lifesavers worked frantically, they became at times, frustrated in their efforts, as repeatedly the bodies of the dead were tossed upon the jagged rocks, and beaten, only to be taken back into the ocean once again by the tides. One Cohasset man, Charles Studley, who lived nearby at Sandy Cove, was almost drowned himself, and had to be pulled from the sea. After his near-death experience, Mr. Studley plunged right back into his gruesome task. A railroad conductor, only known as Mr. Holmes, busied himself all day, comforting the living and pulling the dead out of the water.

One passenger, found clinging to a piece of the ship's wreckage, floated up on some rocks. He was so far gone that he couldn't, or wouldn't, let go of the piece of wreckage he clung to so desperately. Someone finally jumped on it, until it snapped, put a rope around the poor fellow, and pulled him safely to shore. He had passed away, and his look was the face of death personified; a purplish face, his mouth agape, gnarling teeth, and blank, dead, doll eyes, that stared vacantly into nothingness. It was now a familiar look, a look that would not soon be forgotten.

Patrick Sweeney, late of Galway, Ireland, had drowned carrying his 3-year old daughter, Agnes. His wife and ten other children also perished that day. One of the surviving passengers recognized Mrs. Sweeney's remains that afternoon. Her features appeared calm and placid, as if she were in a sweet slumber. She hadn't taken that bad a beating compared to many of the passengers. Many of the dead and the living had taken a brutal beating on the way in to shore.

By nightfall the beach and the rocks around it, all the way down to Whitehead, were strewn with dead bodies, wreckage, and the passenger's personal belongings, all of which had been brutalized. At this point only 25 bodies, dead bodies, had been recovered. However, there were still many stuck in the deadly grasp of the sea, taunting those on shore, perhaps beckoning them as Ahab had his men, to come and join them in death. A watch was set overnight, in hopes of recovering the dead, and hopefully some living.

By October 9, word of the disaster that had befallen the St. John had spread, and people, in throngs, came to see for themselves the results of the shipwreck. The English consul, a Mr. Elliot, when he heard of the disaster, and without prompting, proceeded to Cohasset to render any aid that might be required.

On the train south were many Irish men and women, the friends and relatives of the living and the dead of the St. John. They'd come to Cohasset to identify the remains of their friends and loved ones. Moreover, there were always the curious and morbid.

The Irish community was stunned. Questions were asked: Who was expected? Who was on board the St. John? Who were those drowned? Friends comforted neighbors, who knew they might have lost someone on the wreck.

For now, the people of Cohasset undertook their sorrowful tasks: identifying the bodies of the dearly departed, assisting the survivors, and tending to the funeral that was scheduled for that same day. Throngs crowded the beach now, and soon the shocked and devastated families and friends of the deceased began to arrive. On a small rise, steps from the boiling seas, sat the rough-pine boxes in which the dead were being placed. In some boxes lay one or more children; perhaps they were family. In another lay a parent and child. The sisters of Peggy Adams, and her husband, both of South Boston, found Mrs. Adams in one of the boxes. Their grief was such that it overwhelmed many of those present: such a melancholy meeting after so many months of glee-filled anticipation. One of the boxes contained the remains of Peggy Mullen, her child, and her sister. Mary Joice and her child, John Dolan and his wife, were together now for eternity. Patrick Sweeney, his 3-year old daughter, Agnes, his wife, and their ten other children, were placed in one box. Many of the boxes contained only one body. Soon, these farmers, who'd be burying the dead, nailed down the coffin lids, and marked in chalk, the names of those enclosed, if the names were known. It was now two days aft-er the wreck, and the seas were still pounding wildly off the granite coast of this peaceful fishing community.

These rough-pine boxes were then placed on wagons, and the mourning procession made its way towards the common grave where these immigrants would lay together for eternity. First, the procession made its way to the Unitarian Church on the Common, where services were held. Rev. Joseph Osgood and Rev. Reed said the Mass. At the cemetery, the service was said by Father Rodden, the Catholic priest of Quincy.

Throngs of people crowded the Cohasset shoreline that horrible Sunday, as well as Monday and Tuesday. For a week, the curious and the bereaved made the sad trek, hoping to find the body of a loved one, a friend, or just to observe. The sea, however, gives up its bounty slowly; eventually forty-five bodies would be recovered. Some had solace, others never would.

# CHAPTER FOURTEEN
## "THE SHIPWRECK"

FROM THE BOOK ENTITLED "CAPE COD"
BY HENRY DAVID THOREAU

This story on the St. John was first published in the June 1855 edition of Putnam's Magazine. After Thoreau's death, in 1862, it became Chapter One of his book, Cape Cod.

Much has been written about the wreck of the St. John; songs, poems and stories. Perhaps no one put pen to paper and described the scene in Cohasset, better than Henry David Thoreau. So, at this time, I will let Thoreau speak for me. Here, in part, are chapters taken from his book "Cape Cod," entitled "The Shipwreck," and "Highland Light."

And I quote. "We found many Irish in the cars, going to identify the bodies and to sympathize with the survivors, and also to attend the funeral which was to take place in the afternoon – and when we arrived in Cohasset, it appeared that nearly all the passengers were bound for the beach, which was about a mile distant, and many others…were flocking in from the neighboring countryside. There were several hundreds of them streaming over the Cohasset Common in that direction, some on foot and some in wagons…" Those close to the harbor walked to Atlantic Avenue, and then to the beach.

"As we passed the graveyard we saw a large hole, like a cellar, freshly dug there, and just before reaching the shore, by a pleasantly winding and rocky road, we met several hay-riggings and farm wagons coming away towards the meetinghouse, each loaded with three large, rough-deal boxes. We did not need to ask what was in there. The owners of the wagons were made the undertakers. Many horses and carriages were fastened to the fences near the shore, and, for a mile or more, up and down, the beach was covered with people looking out for bodies, and examining the fragments of the wreck. There was a small island called Brook Island with a hut on it, lying just off shore. This is said to be the rockiest shore in Massachusetts, from Nantasket to Scituate - hard sientic rocks, which the waves have laid bare, but have not been able to crumble. It has been the scene of many a shipwreck.

"The brig St. John, from Galway, Ireland, laden with emigrants, was wrecked on Sunday morning; it was now Tuesday morning, and the sea was still breaking violently on the rocks. There were eighteen or twenty of the same large boxes that I have mentioned, laying on a green hillside, a few rods from the water, and surrounded by a crowd. The bodies that had been recovered, twenty-seven or eight in all, had been collected there. Some were rapidly nailing down the lids, which were yet loose, and peeping under cloths, for each body, with such rags as still adhered to it, was covered loosely with a white sheet. I witnessed no signs of grief, but there was a sober dispatch of business, which was affecting. One man was seeking to identify a particular body, and one undertaker or carpenter was calling to another to know what box a certain child was put.

"I saw many marbled feet and matted heads as the cloths were raised, and one livid, swollen, and mangled body of a drowned girl - who probably had intended to go out to service in some American family - to which rags still adhered, with a string, half concealed by the flesh about its swollen neck; the coiled up wreck of a human hulk, gashed by the rocks or fishes, so that the bone and muscle were exposed, but quite bloodless - nearly red and white - with wide-open and staring eyes, yet lusterless, dead-lights; or like the cabin windows of a stranded vessel, filled with sand. Sometimes there were two or more children, or a parent and child, in the same box, and on the lid would perhaps be written with red chalk 'Bridget such-a-one, and sister's child.'

"The surrounding sward was covered with bits of sails and clothing. I have since heard, from one who lives by this beach, that a woman who had come over before, but had left her infant behind for her sister to bring, came and looked into these boxes, and saw in one - probably the same whose superscription I have quoted - her child in her sister's arms, as if the sister had meant to be found thus; and within three days after, the mother died from the effect of that sight.

"We turned from this and walked along the rocky shore. In the first cove were strewn what seemed fragments of a vessel, in small pieces mixed with sand and seaweed, and great quantities of feathers; but it looked so old and rusty, that I at first took it to be some old wreck which had lain there many years. I even thought of Captain Kidd, and that the feathers were those which seafowl had cast there and perhaps there might be some tradition about it in the neighborhood. I asked a sailor if that was the St. John, he said it was. I asked him where she struck. He pointed to a rock in front of us, a mile from shore called the Grampus Rock, and added - 'You can see a part of her now sticking up; it looks like a small boat.'

"I saw it. It was thought to be held by the chain-cables and the anchors. I asked if the bodies which I saw were all that were drowned.

"Not a quarter of them" said he.

"Where are the rest?"

"Right under that piece you see."

"It appeared to us that there was enough rubbish to make the wreck of a large vessel in this cove alone, and that it would take many days to cart it off. It was several feet deep, and here and there was a bonnet or a jacket on it. In the very midst of the crowd about this wreck, there were two men with carts busily collecting the seaweed which the storm had cast up, and conveying it beyond the reach of the tide, though they were often obliged to separate fragments of clothing from it, and they might at any moment have found a human body under it. Drown who might; they did not forget that this weed was a valuable manure. This shipwreck had not produced a visible vibration in the fabric of society.

"About a mile south we could see, rising above the rocks, the masts of the British brig the St. John had endeavored to follow, which had slipped her cables, and, by good luck, run into the mouth of Cohasset Harbor. A little further along the shore we saw a man's clothes on a rock; further, a woman's scarf, a gown, a straw bonnet, the brig's caboose, and one of her masts high and dry, broken into several pieces. In another rocky cove, several rods from the water, and behind rocks twenty feet high, lay a part of one side of the vessel, still hanging together. It was perhaps forty feet long, by fourteen feet wide.

"I was even more surprised at the power of the waves, exhibited on this shattered frag-ment, than I had been at the sight of the smaller fragments before. The largest timbers and iron braces were broken superfluously, and I saw that no material could withstand the power of the waves; that iron must go to pieces in such a case, and an iron vessel would be cracked up like an eggshell on the rocks. Some of these timbers, however, were so rotten that I could almost thrust my umbrella through them. They told us that some were saved on this piece and showed where the sea had heaved it into this cove, which was now dry. When I saw where it had come in, and in what condition, I wondered that any had been saved.

"A little further on a crowd of men were collected around the mate of the St. John, who was telling his story. He was a slim-looking youth, who spoke of the captain as the Master, and seemed a little excited. He was saying that when they jumped into the boat, she filled, and, the vessel lurching, the weight of the water in the boat caused the painter to break, and so they were separated. Whereat one man came away saying, 'Well I don't see but he tells a straight enough story. You see the weight of the water in the lifeboat broke the painter. A boat full of water is very heavy,' and so on, in a loud and impertinently earnest tone, as if he had a bet depending on it, but had no humane interest in the matter. Another, a large man, stood nearby upon a rock, gazing into the sea, and chewing a large quid of tobacco, as if that habit were forever confirmed with him.

"Come," says another to his companions, "let's be off. We've seen the whole of it. It's no use to stay to the funeral.

"Further we saw one standing upon a rock, who, we were told, was one that was saved. He was a sober-looking man, dressed in a jacket and grey pantaloons, with his hands in the pockets. I asked him a few questions, which he answered; but her seemed unwilling to talk about it, and soon walked away. By his side stood one of the lifeboat men, in an oilcloth jacket, who told us how they went to the relief of the British brig, thinking that the boat of the St. John, which they passed on the way, held all her crew - for the waves prevented their seeing those who were on the vessel, though they might have saved some had they known there were any there. A little further was the flag of the St. John spread on a rock to dry, and held down by stones at the corners. This frail, but essential and significant portion of the vessel, which had so long been the sport of the winds, was sure to reach shore. There were one or two houses visible from these rocks, in which some of the survivors were recovering from the shock, which their bodies and minds had sustained. One was not expected to live.

"We kept on down the shore as far as a promontory called Whitehead, that we might see more of the Cohasset Rocks. In a little cove, within half a mile, there were an old man and his son collecting, with their team, the seaweed which that fatal storm had cast up, as serenely employed as if there had never been a wreck in the world, though they were within sight of the Grampus Rock, on which the St. John had struck. The old man had heard that there was a wreck and knew most of the particulars, but he said that he had not been up there since it happened. It was the wrecked weed that concerned him most, rockweed, kelp, and seaweed, as he named them, which he had carted to his barnyard; and those bodies were to him but other weeds, which the tide cast up, but which were of no use to him. We afterwards came to the lifeboat in its harbor, waiting for another emergency - and in the afternoon we saw the funeral procession at a distance, at the head of which walked the captain with the other survivors.

"On the whole, it was not so impressive a scene as I might have expected. If I had found one body cast upon the beach in some lonely place, it would have affected me more. I sympathized rather with the winds and waves, as if to toss and mangle these poor humans' bodies was the order of the day. If this was the Law of Nature, why waste anytime in awe or pity? If the last day were come, we should not think so much about the separation of friends or the blighted prospects of individuals. I saw that corpses might be multiplied, as on the field of battle, till they no longer affected us in any degree, as exceptions to the common lot of humanity. Take all the graveyards together, they are always the majority.

"It is the individual and private that demands our sympathy. A man can attend but one funeral in the course of his life, can behold but one corpse. Yet I saw that the inhabitants of the shore would be not a little affected by this event. They would watch there many days and nights for the sea to give up its dead, and their imaginations and sympathies would supply the place of mourners far away, who as yet knew not of the wreck. Many days after this, something white was seen floating on the water by one who was sauntering the beach. It was approached in a boat, and found to be the body of a woman, which had risen in an upright position, whose white cap was blown back with the wind. I saw that the beauty of the shore itself was wrecked for many a lonely walker there, until they could perceive, at last, how its beauty was enhanced by wrecks like this, and it acquired thus a rarer and sublime beauty still.

"Why care for these bodies? They really have no friends but the worms or the fishes. Their owners were coming to the New World, as Columbus and the Pilgrims did - they were within a mile of its shores; but before they could reach it, they emigrated to a newer world than ever Columbus dreamed of, yet one of whose existence we believe that there is far more universal and convincing evidence - though it has not yet been discovered by science - than Columbus had of this; not merely mariners tales and some paltry driftwood and seaweed, but a continual drift and instinct to all our shores. I saw their empty hulks that came to land: but they themselves, meanwhile, were cast upon some shore yet further west, toward which we are all tending, and which we shall reach at last, it may be through storm and darkness, as they did. No doubt, we have reason to thank God that they have not been 'shipwrecked into life again.'

"The mariner who makes the safest port in Heaven, perchance, seems to his friends on earth to be shipwrecked, for they deem Boston Harbor the better place; though perhaps invisible to them, a skillful pilot comes to meet him, and the fairest and balmiest gales blow off that coast, his good ship makes the land in halcyon days, and he kisses the shore in rapture there, while his old hulk tosses in the surf here. It is hard to part with one's body, but, no doubt, it is easy enough to do without it when once it is gone. All their plans and hopes burst like a bubble! Infants by the score dashed on the rocks by the enraged Atlantic Ocean! No! No! If the St. John did not make her port here, she has been telegraphed there. The strongest wind cannot stagger a spirit; it is a Spirit's breath. A just man's purpose cannot be split on any Grampus or material rock, but itself will split rocks till it succeeds…

*Paul A. Fiori*

"...This rocky shore is called Pleasant Cove, on some maps; on the map of Cohasset, that name appears to be confined to the particular cove where I saw the wreck of the St. John. The ocean did not look, now, as if any were ever shipwrecked in it; it was not grand and sublime, but beautiful as a lake. Not a vestige of a wreck was visible, nor could I believe that the bones of many a shipwrecked man were buried in that pure sand."

The first paragraph is from Shebnah Rich's book, entitled Truro, Cape Cod: Landmarks and Seamarks. Added at the end is part of the chapter from Thoreau's book Cape Cod entitled Highland Light, and I quote. "Ocean waves [and currents] have a way of moving a body. The brig St. John, from Galway to Boston, with emigrants, was wrecked on the Cohasset Rocks, October, 1849. The bodies of a man and a woman from the wreck were picked up near Highland Light." Thoreau takes over here once again, and I quote. "An inhabitant of Truro, on Cape Cod, told me that about a fortnight after the St. John was wrecked at Cohasset he found two bodies on the shore at the Clay Pounds. They were those of a man and a corpulent woman. The man had thick boots on, though his head was off, but 'it was alongside.' It took the finder some weeks to get over the sight. Perhaps they were a man and wife, and whom God had joined the ocean currents had not put asunder. Yet but what slight accidents at first may they have been associated in their drifting. Some of the bodies of those passengers were picked up far out to sea, boxed up and sunk; some brought ashore and buried. There are more consequences to a shipwreck than the underwriter's notice. The Gulf Stream may return some to their native shores, or drop them in some out-of-the-way wave of ocean, where time and the elements will write new riddles with their bones- but return to land again."

Although the citizens of Cohasset had shown these beaten immigrants kindness and compassion, they still looked at them with a twinge of Yankee disdain, after all they were Irish; an alien people, speaking in an alien tongue - Gaelic. "...They are curious looking objects..." wrote Elizabeth Lothrop, in her diary.

The Pilot, a Catholic newspaper, would report in its October 13, 1849 edition that, "We understand that they were well cared for by the people of Cohasset..."

On the Internet, I found a letter written by a brother, whose name is unknown, to his sister, only identified as Catherine. Here, in part, is some of that letter, and I quote.
"From Cohasset, Massachusetts, October 14, 1849.
"Dearest Catherine,

"Word reached us in Boston through The Boston Pilot newspaper that the John Bull brig St. John had foundered off the coast south of Boston. The brig, it was reported, had been dashed upon the rocks on or around the 9th inst., the victim of yet another terrible nor'easter which plagues this area of the country. Reports determined a second brig, the Kathleen, which had accompanied the St. John, made it with all safety into Cohasset Harbor.
"Upon hearing this news we loaded several trunks with clothing, blankets, whiskey, laudanum, and other sundries we felt would be necessary should the worst be feared. We traveled through Weymouth, two more anxious individuals in a bizarre sea of humanity headed south on a similar endeavour. Nearly all of the others on the road were relatives, or acquaintances of the St. John passengers one way or another. Quite a few had the same idea as we – they brought with them sundries to offer and comfort in the hope the subject of their search was alive.
"It took us almost the whole day before we could arrive in Cohasset proper. The roads were clogged with traffic. People were arriving via packet, the South Shore Railroad and even attempted the stage. Others, with little money in their purses, made their way here in the time-honored manner of pilgrims the world over – their feet. We passed the cemetery on our way into town; a large pit had recently been excavated. Grieving relatives and coffins ringed the perimeter. We watched a fight breakout – some father was convinced one of the coffins held his late sister, another believed it contained his niece.
"The Common was a muddy morass of humanity and bovinity surrounding a somewhat white church. The cows registered the chaos

with detached interest before they wandered off to another part of the Common to continue being cows. Pigs trundled everywhere. Dogs barked like mad. The place reeked of manure. The smell of the seashore, and another scent, one I recognized instantly from my days of clearing greasers from the hovels during the fight in Monterrey two years ago - death accompanied by panic.

"Everyone seemed to head for the beaches, not a mile distant. We followed suit, threading our buggy through town, and out to the shoreline proper. Along the way we could see the distant masts of the Kathleen as she lay at anchor in the ironically-named Pleasant Cove, just outside the main harbor. We passed many wagons loaded with coffins. Some were empty; some were full.

"The Cohasset coastline is composed of what appears at first to be solid granite. The Mother Atlantic flings herself against the rock, and while immediate danger is not seen it is clear that said rock has worn down through the years. There are large cracks which reveal igneous intrusions. There are 'bowls' in the rock, for lack of a better term; indentations which appear to have been scooped out by some bored Promethian hand. We also saw the occasional pool which traps the local sea life in a microcosm of the ocean. These were also natural collection points for the debris of the wreck. The tidal line is demarked with a black stain like a ringworm around a giant's bathtub, and reinforced with seaweed. There are a few beaches, or sandy places, to be had. I am guessing the geography does not allow much deposit of sand, except up the road at the salt works. [What] industry there was, was at a standstill because the residents were combing the coastline for survivors or bodies.

"A careful sweep of the horizon revealed the remains of the St. John still impaled on the rocks. Several longboats were tied alongside, and either [the] passengers remains or possessions were being transferred to be rowed to shore. I spied a spider-like skeletal structure on an outcropping near the wreck. I was told by a local in his queer nasal accent that it was the beginnings of Minot Lighthouse, whose function was to prevent future disasters such as this one. I think I can be forgiven if the phrase 'time and tide wait for no man" crossed my thoughts to be applied liberally to the situation at hand.

*On Grampus Ledge*

"We could hear the distant cries from the saltworks. 'Ho, up here! I think we have found one!'

"Where at?

"Over this way, near the Cove!

"We dogtrotted to the source of the cry. Indeed, the geography of the area left an opening to allow sand to build into a sandbar. It might damage a skiff in the hands of a careless skipper, but not the rowboats presently drug up on to the beach. Several bodies lay at rest underneath tarpaulins. We fling them back. The bodies here were men, women, [and] children; there was no blood. They were all very white except for the wounds which were slightly red and wet. One fellow bent to place coins on the eyelids of a girl. He whispered a prayer, 'Praise God, no Priscilla…'

"I must close for now."

I remain, etc:
Your humble brother.

As I noted earlier, the author of this letter is unknown. The letter is dated a week after the wreck and five or six days after the funeral. It seems that writer was in Cohasset at about the same time as Thoreau. Whoever the author is I would like to thank him.

According to The Registration and Returns of Births, Marriages, and Deaths of Massachusetts 1849, and I quote. "In the return from Cohasset the clerk says: On the 7th of October, 1849, the brig St. Johns (sic) was wrecked on our shore, and about one hundred lives were lost; fifty bodies of which have been collected and buried in our Burying Ground - some in Scituate, some in Hull, and [some] in Boston. These have been omitted in [our previous] report."

Now the Voice spoke wearily.

"They came to see, they came looking for friends and family or what remained of that. They came to give comfort and they came to lay us to rest. The Irish from Boston shaken and weak, shocked at what fate had decreed; the locals were more often than not just curious

"When they arrived the seas were still pounding against this cold, hard, granite coast. Here and there and everywhere lay the shattered pieces of our lives: a scarf, a baby bonnet, a shattered mast. I saw my coffin and the wagon that would haul my dead body away. All around us, the dead, were the living grimly, intently going about their gruesome task, as they searched for a loved one.

"Our bodies, most of them anyway, were now hidden 'neath snowy white sheets. Questions were asked, 'Where is this body, or that one?' Then a sheet would be raised and reveal a now bloodless corpse, with matted hair; it was the puffed, broken body of a once vibrant child whose now lifeless form had been bitten by rocks and fishes, exposing muscle and bone: she stared blankly into nothing. The woman looking for the child, an aunt, fainted at the sight.

"In death I studied these people of Cohasset; the wreck and the death of so many disturbs them little. I supposed that many of them had, for generation after generation, made a living from this sea; they were a compassionless lot. After all, the sea had not changed a lick after it swallowed us up and then regurgitated 145 more victims, as though we were just so many grains of sand, or yet another yard or two of seaweed. Those people saw us as less important than that valuable weed.

"As I look at this seashore there is something of a rare, sublime beauty about it. Even after such a tragic event it retains its beauty, a beauty it might not have had had not the storm that murdered so many, hit at this exact spot." Now the Voice pauses, and then continues, angrily.

"Who are these Cohasset men that play at saving lives? Was it not their job to help those in distress; weren't they lifesavers? To us who have moved on to a far better place than here, they were useless – they are irrelevant! How did they fare yesterday in their battle against nature's force? Where were they while we were being beaten against the Grampus Ledge? Where were they when we needed them most?" I'll tell you where they were!

"Offshore there was a second ship, riding easily on those angry waters in the harbor. Luckily this ship instead of beating itself senseless until its death on those rocks along this foul coast, slipped easily into this well-protected harbor. Instead of coming to our rescue, as we were dying out there on the Grampus, the fine, brave lifesavers of Cohasset went to save the crew of that other ship – that ship was never in danger.

Yet that ships crew and its few passengers; I think I counted ten in all, are all alive today, while 145 of us, those on board the St. John, perished! Lifesavers! Ha! The only people the brave lifesavers of Cohasset save yesterday were those who did not need saving ! So much for the good man does for his fellow man!

"I spoke to one of those lifesavers; 'we never saw your boat,' he told me sadly. 'We were not negligent in our duty,' he argued half-heartedly. 'The waves...the waves were just too high. We saw the lifeboat and thought...' and his voice trailed away, as his head dropped to his chest.

"It was your job, a job you'd chosen. You chose to help...and you didn't, I said to him quietly.

# CHAPTER FIFTEEN
## FUNERAL AND MASSES:

There were three services held the day of the funeral. Two were held on Cohasset Common at the Unitarian Church. Masses were said by the Reverend Joseph Osgood and Reverend Frederick Reed, both of Cohasset; a Catholic service was said at the cemetery, by Father John J. Rodden, of Quincy, Massachusetts.

From 1842-1898, Osgood served as the minister of the Unitarian Church in Cohasset. He was a long-time friend of author and Transcendentalist Henry David Thoreau, both men having courted Miss Ellen Sewell, who was now Mrs. Joseph Osgood. Osgood was also very active in town civic circles.

Reverend Frederick A. Reed usually said his Mass at the Congregational Church, located directly across the street from Osgood's Unitarian Church. He was born in 1821 in Boston, and was a graduate of Amherst College; Class of 1843. After attending the Bangor Theological Seminary, he came to Cohasset. He passed away in 1883, in Harvard, Massachusetts.

Father John J. Rodden, of Quincy, the first Boston-born priest to be educated in Rome, would be the Catholic presence at the Mass. At the time of the wreck, what few Catholics Cohasset had had always gone to Quincy to hear their Mass, or to the home of Michael Neptune Brennock, on Border Street. After the wreck of the St. John, these few Catholics went to Quincy, asking that Father Rodden officiate at the Mass and burial of the Irish-Catholics that had died in the wreck. Father Rodden carried himself and his faith well, and gave a sermon that was well remembered for many years. Rodden would eventually give the first Catholic Mass ever said in Cohasset, in a church.

Hundreds of people attended all of the masses. People came from Boston, Cohasset, Hingham, Scituate, and Hull. When the masses were ended, the funeral procession lined up on the common to begin the slow, sad march to Central Cemetery, led by Captain Oliver. With coffin-laden wagons in the fore, the mourners; friends, family, and utter strangers, made the heartbreaking journey to the cemetery, not a quarter-mile away. Upon arriving they beheld the final resting place of the forty-five souls, whose battered and beaten bodies had been recovered: a 25x9x6 foot hole. The spot chosen was lovely: it looked out on Little Harbor and the Atlantic Ocean. Sadly, more bodies would come ashore in different locations; they'd be buried not with their fellow travelers, but alone, in anonymity.

To this day, the actual site of the grave is unknown. Its exact location has never been marked, or recorded. It is supposed that the grave lies near the grave of Hugo Ormo, a local restaurant owner, but this has never been verified (More on this subject in Appendix B of this book).

Perhaps these unfortunates were in a better life now. Most of them were probably in a weakened condition after such a voyage. When the ship was caught up in the storm, they were probably in no shape to help themselves, or anyone else for that matter.

In Ireland, they'd survived An Gorta Mor. They had fled their homeland and that horrid existence in hopes of a better, happier, and healthier life; as they boarded the ship, they were shells. Throw in a long trip on board a creaky, leaky boat, bad food, fetid air, and the threat of disease, and we can only wonder at their physical and mental conditions. I imagine you'd have to live through it yourself to fully understand. Just imagine having so much hope, only to have it dashed away by such an unexpected event, on the very coast of that land of hope and promise. Those who perished that day will never be forgotten. They had left a land of famine, in search of a land of hope. Too much praise can never be given to the courageous citizens of Cohasset, for their conduct during the whole tragic event.

Notice To Mariners
Customs House, Boston
October 9, 1849

The lighthouse on Minot's Ledge, Cohasset, is nearly completed and will probably be ready for lighting in a few weeks. We trust that the official notice will be given as soon as practicable, when it is ready.

H. Greeley, Jr.
Superintendent of Lights

In its October 13th issue, The Pilot, a Catholic newspaper, ran a three-column story on the wreck. Accompanying the story was a list of the passengers and crew, deceased and living, as had been identified at that time. The next week, on the 20th, and three weeks later, the paper added to the list, and made note of the services rendered both the living and the dead, by the people of Cohasset.

On October 29, 1849, the weather was pleasant. Out at Boston Light, Lucy Maria Long was walking along the island's shore when…"I saw the body of a man on the bar. [We] supposed it had washed up from the wreck of the vessel lost on Minot's Ledge…" Bodies washed up days later, near Pleasant Beach, Cohasset. Bodies would continue to wash up from Boston to Cape Cod, in the next few months.

Notice to Mariners
Customs House, Boston
November 25, 1849

The light recently erected on Minot's Ledge, is now so far completed that it has been determined to exhibit a fixed beacon thereon, of the 1st Order, on or after the evening of January 1, 1850. Minot's Ledge, or the Cohasset Rocks, is 8 miles SE ½ E from Boston Light, and consists of 15 rocks, out of water, and ledges all around them, extending N and S from 3 to 4 miles. The depth of the water around the rocks is 5-6 fathoms. When the light shall be in operation, Scituate Light, which is 6 miles S of Cohasset rocks, showing two lights, one red and one white, will be suspended by order of the department. Masters of vessels, pilots, and other persons interested, are required to take special notice thereof.

H. Greeley, Jr.
Superintendent of Lights

# CHAPTER SIXTEEN
## THE CELTIC CROSS

Now the voice speaks softly, mournfully.

"All that's left is this Stone Cross, yet even that cold piece of America can tell our story; the story of the Irish. It speaks of a wind so wild and furious; of the storm, that nor'easter, that carried us away; of the waves that hurled us, like a single piece of paper, onto Grampus Ledge; of an ocean that ate us up, then spat us to shore – some of us lived that horribly sad October morn.

"Our memorial sits on a slight rise in this graveyard, its pointed shaft reaching to the heavens, as it looks out over Little Harbor, Sandy Beach, and the Atlantic Ocean. There are no names, only a date, and words to remember those of us who perished so close to fulfilling our dreams, only to be taken by the sea: that merciless foe.

" This stone will talk of our courage, through it all; of the strength and will of those not taken away; of the Irish spirit – of all who sailed on the brig St. John."

On Memorial Day, 1914, The Ancient Order of Hibernians, and its Ladies Auxiliary, participated in the dedication of a 20-ft. tall, Celtic Cross in Cohasset's Central Cemetery.

Thomas DeSantis wrote those words explaining the origins of the Celtic Cross, and I quote. "They originated when Ireland was under Viking occupation, as a symbol of the Irish peoples will to survive any occupation. They were immovable, unburnable, and stood as the symbol of the Irish resolve to preserve their heritage and their religion..."

The sculptor of the Cross was P.J. Tagney. It is approximately 18x4.5x4.5 feet. It's base is 1.25x6x6 feet. It is an elaborately carved Celtic Cross adorned on the front with the seal of the Ancient Order of Hibernians; which consists of clasped hands, a harp, a rising sun, ivy, and shamrocks. On the back of the Cross is another seal of the A.O.H. which consists of clasped hands, a harp, ivy, and shamrocks.

The principal speaker that day was Massachusetts Governor, David I. Walsh. The Cross was unveiled by Miss Theresa C. St. John, of Cohasset, the granddaughter of Mary and James St. John. The religious presence was provided by Father Farragh Brogan, Pastor of St. Anthony's Parish. Over 7,000 Hibernians from all over the state attended the event.

The inscription on the Cross reads: "This cross was erected and dedicated to mark the final resting place of about forty-five Irish Emigrants from a total company of ninety-nine who lost their lives on Grampus Ledge off Cohasset, October 7, 1849, in the wreck of the Brig St. John, from Galway, Ireland: R.I.P."

Former Mayor of Boston John "Honey Fitz" Fitzgerald, commenting on the commemoration of the shipwreck, and I quote. "Though it is a tragic event we observe, it was indeed the symbol of one of the greatest contributions made to the United States - the tide of Irish immigration which did much to make us strong."

One hundred years after the wreck, in 1949, Archbishop Richard J. Cushing, later Richard Cardinal Cushing, Archbishop of Boston, said a solemn Pontifical Mass on the grounds of St. Anthony's Catholic Church, in Cohasset. This was done in memory of the St. John's victims, and to commemorate the first Catholic Mass ever said in Cohasset. Cushing had begun his priesthood at St. Anthony's Parish in 1921.

Among those clergy in attendance were Rev. Michael J. Houlihan, Pastor of St. Patrick's Church in Watertown, he was also the Chaplain of the Ancient Order of Hibernians; Rev. Thomas A. Flynn, Pastor of St. Angela's of Mattapan, these two men were the deacons of honor. Rev. Michael J. Splaine, of St. Mary's in Brookline gave the sermon.

According to an article about the services, written in The Boston Herald, on August 7, 1949, and I quote. "…assisting will be Rev. Frederick McManus: Master of Ceremonies, Rt. Rev. P.J. Waters, and

Rev. William J. Desmond; a Cohasset resident. Rev. Ralph Grimes, Rev. Joseph Daley, Rev. Joseph W. Leahy, Rev. Francis Kearney, Rev. Lawrence Crowley, Rev. Ralph Enos; a Cohasset resident, Rev. Edward Tangney, Rev. Martin Haney, S.J., Rev. James Cassidy, Rev. John W. Mahoney, Rev. Patrick J. Flaherty, and Mr. Francis Regan, will also participate."

Today, residents of Ireland, Irish-Americans, and many others stop by and pay their respects at the 20-ft. Celtic Cross. Some may actually be relatives of those who lived and died on Grampus Ledge, October 7, 1849.

To celebrate the 140th anniversary of the wreck, the Cohasset Historical Society, with the assistance of the AOH of Massachusetts, and the Irish National Grave Association, held ceremonies in Cohasset, and laid a wreath at the foot of the Cross.

On June 28, 1998, a Sunday, the Boston Famine Memorial was unveiled. Among the list of dignitaries on hand for the event, was a quiet, handsome, unassuming young man from Cohasset, Massachusetts. Martin St. John, the great-great-great grandson of Mary St. John, read the commemorative plague, honoring the dead of the St. John.

October 10, 1999 – On this day, 150 years after the tragedy in which ninety-nine Irish emigrants drowned off Cohasset, residents of Ireland and the United States have gathered to mark that sad day. Hundreds have joined together to participate in ceremonies over this weekend. Bernard Cardinal Law, Archbishop of Boston, celebrated a memorial mass at St. Anthony's Church, in Cohasset, in remembrance.

Ninety-nine Irish emigrants, and this number has always been in dispute, died off Cohasset, while most of the crew survived by scrambling into the only lifeboat available. Sean Lynch, 55, of Ireland, had relatives who were part of the ship's crew, and survived. "Two crew members, Martin O'Flaherty, 19, and his brother, James, 21, returned home, but that day and that wreck were never subjects to be discussed," stated Lynch. "It was Irish custom not to talk about such things," he said in closing.

*Paul A. Fiori*

According to the website, clanhannon.com, another monument, or if you wish, memorial, can be seen on Gorumna Island, Co. Galway, Ireland. Sitting on the water's edge, passerby's may stop and read these words, in Gaelic of course.

In domos do na fir,
Na mna
Agus Na paisti as
Lartar na Heiteann
A batad nuair a bris
An 'Brig St. John'
Ar costa
Cohasset, Boston
An qu
Deiread Fomair 1849
Suainneas Siorai

or in English

In homage to the men,
the women
and the children of Ireland
onboard the breakup of
'The Brig St. John'
Upon the coast
Cohasset, Boston
The 9th
October 1849
Eternal Rest

And I questioned the voice as we stood at the cross.

"What are you thinking?" I asked. "Why do you stand at this cross?" I wondered. "Are you thinking of what might have been; of bright futures dashed to pieces on our Sleeping Whales; of dreams now wasted; of hope forlorn; of all that and so much more within your sight, your grasp, only to be wrenched from your hands so close to being?

"Can you recall those friends that made the trip with you? Do you think of the families who remain, yet heart broken? Are you thinking of all those who never touched land again in life; who never saw their dreams fulfilled; whose hopes lay in pieces on our shore? Tell me spirit, tell them, what are you thinking?" The voice had to reply.

"We cannot think of the past, that is gone, and cannot be recaptured, only recalled. You must live in the present, the now, and ask yourself; what can I do? "Why does one person live and the other die? Why do you live in the past, while I, even in death, think of what can be done now, or in the days, months, and years to come? What does one life mean to another; what is that one life really worth?

"I think all that has happened, and all that will happen is a part of the Almighty's grand plan," stated the voice. "Only He lives eternally; He lives in Heaven and on Earth, this much I know; as should you. In spirit form even I am a part of that plan; this was foretold. You are alive, and yet, he has plans for you and your mortal friends: you are all a part of the plan." And the voice paused.

"So I say to you, now: dream! Dream the things we cannot; see things that we can no longer see! Look to a future that is no longer ours, but is still limitless: it is all a part of His plan."

# CHAPTER SEVENTEEN
## QUESTIONS:

Why not find a safe harbor? Capt. Oliver noted, when passing Cape Cod Light, that the "…weather was thick, with a light SE breeze;" this was at 5 p.m., on October 6. Eight hours later, at 1 a.m., the St. John is off Scituate Light, at Cedar Point. By now, the winds had shifted slightly to the NE and were blowing hard. Why didn't he, at this time, turn his ship west and make for the shelter of Scituate Harbor, instead of beating his ship towards Boston?

Scituate Harbor is now and was then wider, deeper, larger, and much less treacherous to enter than Cohasset Harbor, and would've provided ample shelter from the storm. Choosing to press on proved Oliver's folly - at a deadly cost.

Were Capt. Oliver and his crew drunk? Perhaps drunk is too harsh a term to use, under the circumstances. Instead, I'll rephrase the question and ask; were they hung over? What is known is this.

Once the St. John cleared Cape Cod Light, Oliver called all of the passengers on deck and gave them they joyous news that this was going to be their final night on the ship. He then had "…a treat of ardent spirits" given to the passengers, crew, and himself, in celebration. All on board then made merry for the rest of the evening. How much did the captain and crew drink? I know many people who make their living on the sea, and they can put away quite a bit of "ardent spirit." Perhaps the crew enjoyed themselves a bit too much. If they were hung over or even worse, intoxicated, it would have affected their actions, slowing them, thus making Grampus Ledge an unavoidable obstacle.

Why didn't Captain Oliver remain with his ship? So much of what Capt. Oliver did, from Cape Cod to the Grampus remains questionable. I have no idea if there is a steadfast naval or maritime rule or law regarding the order in which people are to be taken off an endangered ship. What I have heard is this - women and children first, and the captain last. How many sea captains have gone down gloriously with their ships? I have no idea. However, Oliver's actions once the St. John struck the Grampus seem reprehensible.

Oliver and those members of his crew that survived seem only to be concerned with their own welfare. When the jollyboat snapped it bolts and fell into the water, Oliver and many of his crew were in it before it swamped and sank. After being pulled from the water by his 1st mate, he is next seen in the longboat, and then safely on shore at the Glades, in Scituate.

No one can change history we can only examine it and ask questions. We will never know how many people could have been saved had the jollyboat not swamped; we do know that twenty-five died trying to get into it, causing it to swamp. We will never know how many could have been saved if Oliver and his crew had not taken the longboat away. Although his own life was spared, as well as some of the crew, and two passengers, Oliver should have done the right thing, the honorable thing, and stayed with his ship. Maybe, because of the situation, what he did could not be avoided - or perhaps he was just a coward!

From The History of Norfolk County, Massachusetts, by D.H. Hurd, and I quote. "In contrast to the kindness and heroism shown that day, was the heartlessness of the captain of the St. John, who, with his crew, left the vessel in a boat only half-full, and who in his cruel cowardice, neglected to inform the crew of the life-boat that his wrecked vessel was filled with perishing men, women, and children..."

Did Capt. Oliver ever speak with the members of the Cohasset Lifeboat? What is known is that they passed each other somewhere between the Grampus and the Glades. According to Captain Daniel Lothrop's written account of the lifeboats efforts that day, they saw the longboat, but no words were ever passed between the two.

*Paul A. Fiori*

We do know, now, thanks to David Wadsworth, Curator of the Cohasset Historical Society, that the lifesavers apparently never saw the St. John, and would have attempted a rescue there if they had.

What about the Kathleen? According to David Wadsworth, Curator of the Cohasset Historical Society, the Kathleen was stuck near Briggs Harbor, or perhaps Bassing Beach. Bassing Beach seems impossible because the St. John could not have seen the ship if it were that far into the harbor, due to the weather. The Kathleen had not struck bottom, apparently, yet she was flying her distress flags; her colors at half-mast, her Union down, which may have led the men in the lifeboat to think the ship was sinking. She had dragged her anchor however, and was being pushed closer to the shore. The men in the lifeboat pulled towards her, and were soon along side of her. Somehow, the Kathleen managed to avoid any of the Cohasset Rocks. It was now about 11:30 A.M. The Kathleen's captain implored those in the lifeboat to save his passengers; five children were put into the lifeboat safely. Soon enough the great ship began to drift once again. She struck a bar, and lost her rudder. The Kathleen came to rest in Brigg's Harbor.

Who stole the Captain's Desk? This question is partially answered in a letter written by Lucy E. Treat, and found in the Archives of the Cohasset Historical Society, and reprinted here courtesy of The Cohasset Historical Society, and I quote.

"On the morning after the British brig St. John, loaded with Irish immigrants from Galway, Ireland, had been driven by a northeast gale upon Grampus Ledge off Cohasset, my father (Nathaniel Treat) was cruising the beaches in the Sandy Cove area. As he rounded Lyman's Point, he saw a neighbor pull a chest up in the bushes and hide it. [He also had in his possession a fine new quadrant]. That winter the latter payed off the mortgage on his house, and seemed able to afford unusual luxuries.

"Two generations later, this man's grandson gave to my brother a small portable writing desk, such as a captain's usually used onboard ships. He said that his grand-father had found it on the morning after the wreck of the ship St. John.

"A ship's money was at that time carried in gold, since there is in the desk a secret drawer, the supposition is that there was money in that chest, when found by the grand-father."

Was Capt. Oliver ever investigated? It has been reported that an inquest was held, and a verdict rendered in accordance with the facts given. However, after the funeral he seems to have vanished. In his report of the disaster, Oliver wrote, and I quote. "Saturday 5 p.m., we passed Cape Cod with a light SE wind: weather thick; hove to with head to the NE; at 4 a.m., wore ship and stood south; at 630 a.m., made Minot's Ledge. Not having room to wear ship, ventured to run where we saw a brig at anchor inside of the light. The violence of the gale and heavy sea caused us to drag our anchors, when we cut away the masts, and held on for a shore (sic) [short] time. The gale increased, she dragged again, struck and thumped heavily for about an hour before she broke up. Previous to breaking up the jolly boat was hanging by the tackles along side, when the stern ringbolt broke, and the boat fell into the water. The captain, second mate, and two boys jumped into her to clear her, when about twenty-five passengers jumped in and swamped her. The passen-gers, together with the second mate and boys perished. The captain caught a rope hanging over the quarter, and was drawn on board by the first mate. The long boat was got clear soon after and a heavy sea coming on board, cleared her from the vessel, when a number of passengers jumped over to swim to her, but all perished. The captain, 1st mate (Mr. Cummerford), eight of the crew, and two passengers swam to the boat, and reached shore in safety. The others, seven men and 8 women, came ashore on a part of the deck. The total loss of life: 99 saved, and 21 saved. Twenty five bodies have been washed ashore, this morning." He tells us nothing more.

Who manned the Cohasset Lifeboat? We do know that one person on the lifeboat was Captain Daniel Lothrop, and it is possible that Michael Neptune Brennock was also in the lifeboat, as well as Caleb Lothrop.

Where is the exact location of the grave? According to Robert Fraser, late curator of the Cohasset Historical Society, and I quote. "To this day the grave has never been marked. In fact, it does not appear on any map of Central Cemetery…," this according to a letter written by Fraser to Lt. Cmdr. Niall Brunicardi. It is rumored that the gravesite is located somewhere near the grave of Hugo Ormo, owner and founder of the internationally known Hugo's Restaurant, on Cohasset Harbor.

I always went by the assumption that no one knew the exact location of the grave. It was on Easter Sunday, April 8, 2007, that I learned something that gave me pause to reconsider my thinking.

I had just finished having breakfast at The Silver Spoon Café, in downtown Cohasset, and was in the process of paying my bill; the waitress just happened to be my daughter, so I knew I had to tip her well. While chatting with my daughter, and the café's owner and chef, a fine fellow named Jack, a customer entered the premises. He was there to pick an order to go, and as we stood there, we started to chat lightly. "I am planning to write a letter to your folks concerning the wreck of the St. John," I told him.

He smiled broadly, and replied, "Do it. My folks have a lot of information on the wreck and especially about Mary Kane. They also have a lot of pictures too," he said proudly. "You should go right to the house," he said, "They'll talk all day about that if you want to listen," and he smiled.

"I'm writing a book about the wreck, and it is also a chapter in another book I'm writing on shipwrecks off Cohasset," I told him. "I've been trying to contact anyone that can help me on this. I have addresses of people in Ireland; different historical societies; and some e-mail addresses, it's going to be a long road I think," and I paused, before continuing. "I have found some relatives of survivors over in Ireland, in Vermont, and in Colorado also. Still, I need more on Mary Kane, and on Captain Oliver. Oliver appears to be the most elusive," and I laughed.

"Mary Kane-Cole married my great-great-great grandfather, James St. John," he stated. I was aware of that so I probed a bit.

"What ever happened to Captain Oliver?" I asked. "Wasn't his first name, Martin?"

He looked at me, smiled, and replied. "My uncle was named Bob Oliver. He married my mom's sister. They live in Hull. He is related to Captain Oliver somehow," here he paused, and moved on. "The day the shipwrecked he took off like a coward. Whatever happened to the captain going down with his ship?" he asked angrily, before continuing.

"Every year they have ceremonies remembering the wreck and every year my folks go; and every year [my] Uncle Bob asked if he could go; my dad told him it wouldn't be appropriate!" he said fiercely. Then he said something that threw me for a loop, and sent a chill down my spine.

"You do know that the bodies are not buried under the cross, right?" he asked.

"Yes," I replied.

Then he asked, "Do you know here they are buried?"

"From what I have learned they may be near the grave of Hugo Ormo, the guy that founded Hugo's Lighthouse. No one ever marked the grave, and it is not on any map of the cemetery," I stated.

Again, he smiled, as if he held the secret of the ages in his hands. "My mother took me to the actual site a few years ago," he said quietly. "Ed Tower showed her the location many years ago, and it is not in the cemetery at all. It may have been at one time, but not anymore. It is in the backyard of the house right next door to the cemetery. They were buried in a trench right there, and the family that lives in that house probably has no idea what is buried in their backyard. If you'd like, I can show it to you someday," too which I agreed, immediately. With those words, I bade farewell to Brendan St. John.

There is another story about this unmarked grave that bears telling. I do not know if it is the truth or fiction, but it appears to make perfect sense.

Cohasset, at the time was as Waspish a community as Boston. The Brennock family, living at the harbor, was one of the few Catholic families in town. The story I have heard is this: since the deceased of the St. John were for the most part Catholic, and there was no Catholic burial ground in town, the bodies had to buried in Cohasset's Central Cemetery, the burial ground for what we might call today, the towns "swamp Yankees." Perhaps the town fathers did not want it known that they had desecrated their own holy ground with the souls of Catholics, and that is the reason the gravesite was never marked.

What was the name of the baby given to the Goves, and had been saved by Mr. Lothrop? Who watched from the Glades? What did Captain Oliver do in Scituate? I have no answers to these questions at this time.

In 1850, the Massachusetts Humane Society awarded to the six men who manned the Cohasset Lifesaving Boat that horrible night, $30.00, or $5.00 apiece, for their efforts in saving the crew of the brig St. John. The Society was mistaken, for it was the crew of the Kathleen, they'd saved. One of those receiving a medal was Michael Neptune Brennock.

"One who visits the St. John grave, may find it hard to fend off a feeling of melancholy at the thought of so many winsome, trustful young women…so many strong-bodied, sturdy young men in the bloom of youth, cut off from life at the very threshold of their hopes and expectations." – William J. Loughran –

And now The Voice spoke thoughtfully.

"She sailed from a dark and desperate land, a land of famine, death, and disease. To a new and better world she was bound and all who sailed that day were free of care. Over rough seas and under dark skies, their beating hearts did glow. With faith did we Irish pilgrims sail.

"Soon, the Irish coast was a thing of the past, as the ship sailed to the west, and America. We prayed as the sun went down on another day, and those prayers drifted o'er the ocean, only to be swallowed by the darkness. To the west and America they looked, these men, women, and children of Erin. And they dreamt of freedom, and well-being in a new land: and the night wore on.

"The ship carried them safely through thirty days and nights, carrying their dreams as well. But Fate was also a passenger, and Death his partner; though none knew. These miseries would let us see the Promised Land: and then cast our souls into eternity.

"Many were the hopes and dreams that never came true. Many were the visions that never bore fruit. Many were the lives lost on Grampus Ledge, and on Cohasset's long, rocky shore, we died."

# APPENDIX A
## Reports, Diaries, and Newspaper Articles on the Wreck of the St. John

Articles on the Wreck of the St. John from The Evening Herald (Oct. 8, 1849); The Boston Post (Oct. 9, 1849); The Boston Transcript (Oct. 9, 1849); The Boston Post (Oct. 10, 1849); The Cohasset Town records: Vital Records: Book Two – Births and Deaths (1844-1862). Report written by Newcomb Bates, Jr.; The Wreck of the Immigrant Ship St. John, by Captain Daniel Lothrop, and The St. John Sinking, October 7, 1849, by Miss Elizabeth Lothrop, are property of the Cohasset Historical Society, and are reprinted here with their permission. The articles from The Alton Telegraph and Democratic Review and The Burlington Hawkeye, were found at the Clare County Library site on the Internet. The article from the Galway Vindicator was sent to me by the County Clare Library, County Clare, Ireland. The article entitled Disastrous Wreck and Loss of Life, was found on the Internet.

Each article, or partial article, will have its own page, so as to alleviate any confusion. Much of what you will read below is repetitive, but it gives you, the reader, a glimpse into how the event was reported at the time it happened, and how it is looked at today.

The Galway Vindicator
(Undated)
AWFUL SHIPWRECK AT MINOT'S LEDGE
LOSS OF THE ST. JOHN OF GALWAY
ABOUT ONE HUNDRED DROWNED
MEN, WOMEN, AND CHILDREN

And I quote. "We are indebted to our much respected friends the Messrs. Train and Company, the extensive Shipping and Emigration Agents of Liverpool, for the following intelligence, as (sic) also to our valued friend, John Moore, Esq., Post-Office Pack Inspector of Boston, and formerly a citizen of Galway.

"The Brig St. John, Capt. Oliver, from Galway, the property of Mr. H. Cummerford of this town, anchored inside Minot's Ledge, Saturday, September 5th (sic). At about 7 o'clock, A.M., on Sunday morning, she dragged her anchors and struck the rocks.

"The following particulars of her loss, together with that of ninety-nine of her passengers and crew, is gleaned from the various persons who witnessed the disaster.

"The vessel struck at about 7 A.M., yesterday. The scene was witnessed from Glade (sic) House, and is represented to have been terrible. The sea ran mountains high, and as soon as she touched, the waves swept the unfortunate human beings upon her crowded decks by the dozens into the sea. The spectators of this awful sight imagined they could hear the cries of the victims as they were swept away, but as no boat, save the life-boat, could have lived in that gale, it was found impossible to render aid.

"The life-boat left Cohasset early in the morning, and went to the aid of a British brig which was in danger at the mouth of the harbour, and carried her to a place of safety. They did not, however, visit the wreck, supposing that the long-boat, which they met going towards shore, contained all that belonged to her.

"When the St. John struck, her small boat was got ready, but was swamped at the side by the large number jumping into her. Shortly after the long boat broke her fastening, and floated off from the vessel. The captain and several others swam to and got on board of her, and landed in safety near Glade House. The second mate, two men and two boys of the crew were drowned.

"After the ship struck the rocks, she thumped a while, but shortly went to pieces, holding together not more than fifty or sixty minutes. Seven women and three men came ashore on pieces of the wreck, alive, but some very much exhausted. Two dead bodies were also taken from pieces of the wreck.

"Early in the forenoon, the news of the wreck began to spread, and in the afternoon, the shore was lined with people who were active in getting bodies from the surf. Mr. Holmes, a railroad conductor, was busy during the entire day in aiding the living and rescuing the dead bodies from the waves. One man, whose name we did not learn, came near losing his life in rescuing a body from the surf.

"Towards nightfall the bodies began to come ashore, and quite a number were taken from the surf, all, however, dead. Dead bodies were thrown upon the rocks, but before they could be rescued, the sea would carry them back again.

"Quite a number of her passengers, especially women and children, were below when she struck, and were probably drowned there, as a hole was almost constantly thumped in her bottom. The long boat [which] reached the shore in safety, contained, in addition to the captain and crew, only one passenger. Of seven first class passengers, who were all lost, were three girls , the nieces of the owner of the vessel. Great difficulty was experienced in saving those who came ashore on pieces of the wreck, on account of the surf, which would throw them upon the rocks then carry them to sea again. The poor creatures would cling with a death-grasp to the clothes of those who came to rescue them, and were, with difficulty, made to release their hold, even after having reached a place of safety.

"One woman saved was very badly bruised upon the rocks, and it was thought, last night, that she would die, but she is this morning, most comfortable.

"It is stated that one passenger, clinging to a piece of the wreck, floated to the rocks, but was so far gone as to be unable to unclench his hand. Finally, someone jumped on the fragment, made fast a rope to him, and he was got ashore. His face of a deep purple, his open mouth, his fixed teeth, and deathly eyes, formed a sight long to be remembered.

"So far only twenty-six dead bodies have been recovered, but the surf, which yet runs very high, is full of them. Before nightfall many more will doubtless be taken out. The shore is strewed with the baggage of the passengers, all stove to pieces."

LATER ACCOUNTS
(Galway Vindicator)
(Undated)

And I quote. "Captain Oliver and his surviving mate reached this city (Boston) at twelve o'clock. He states that he made Cape Cod Light about 5 o'clock on Saturday evening; Scituate Light near one o'clock, Saturday morning; then stood away to the northward, to clear the land, for about three hours; then, it being about daylight, tacked the ship and stood SSW, weather very thick; he came inside Minot's Light House, and there saw a brig lying at anchor just inside of breakers, at a place called Hocksett (sic) Rock; tried to wear away up to the brig, but found he could not fetch up, and threw over both anchors, which dragged; he then cut away her masts, and she drifted onto Grampus Ledge, where she went to pieces.

"Previous to breaking up, the jolly boat was hanging by the tackle, alongside, when the stern rigging bolt broke, and the boat fell into the water. The captain, second mate, and two boys jumped in to get her clear, when about twenty-five passengers jumped in and swamped her. The twenty-five, together with the second mate and two boys, perished; the captain caught a rope hanging over the quarter, and was drawn on board by the first mate.

When the longboat was got clear a number of passengers jumped over to swim to her, but all perished. The captain, 1st Mate (Mr. Crawford), and seven of the crew swam to and reached the boat.

The brig was in ballast.

All the survivors were taken to Mr. Lathrop's house. They were chilled, bruised, and many of them senseless. Dr. Foster, the able and philanthropic physician of the village, attended them professionally, and it required untiring perseverance and skill to restore them. All but two of them are in a fair way of recovery. Mrs. Quinlan was struck upon the head with a heavy piece of timber, which inflicted a severe wound, and she was otherwise both internally and externally injured. She will, however, speedily recover. Honora Burke is in a more critical situation. She was very severely injured, and the struggle between life and death in her case has been a severe one. She appears much better this morning, and were it not that she is likely to become a mother in a short time, the Doctor could speak confidently in her case.

A watch was set all night on the beach, to rescue what bodies from the water that might be cast ashore.

Mr. Lathrop, at whose house the survivors were taken, relates an incident that is at once touching and affecting. The waves were dashing high before him, and upon their crested top, as they were breaking upon him, he saw what he thought was a small package of goods. While watching to save even this small relic from the doomed vessel, it fell upon him, striking him upon his face. He reached forth his arm and grasped it – when, lo, he held an infant, yet alive. He placed it in safety and that infant is now doing well in the family of a Mr. Gove, in this town.

From further conversation with the passengers and people of the town, it is certain to our mind, that Captain Oliver is liable to severe censure for some parts of his conduct. We would be the last to say one word that would add to the poignancy of his feelings in view of his great disaster; but in a question involving the lives of more than one hundred fellow beings, we are bound to speak faithfully, the truth, as it has been presented to us.

It seems that on the afternoon of Saturday the 6th Inst., he numbered his passengers.

Upwards of one hundred names were borne upon the manifest, or list, as two passengers called it who answered to the call. A line was then drawn across the deck, and between twenty and thirty other names were borne upon a small memorandum book. If the consignee has a duplicate list of passengers he or they should produce it. Unless a complete list can be produced we can never fully ascertain the exact number who perished on board this vessel on the fatal morning of October 9.

It is stated by three of the passengers that, on the afternoon of Saturday after they had made Provincetown Light, the captain mustered his passengers on deck and joyfully assured them that the last night of their confinement on board had arrived. A sad truth and most fearfully realized. His passage had been a good one and he felt elated. The simple and light-hearted passengers in the exuberance of their feelings prepared for an illumination; the deck and rigging were decorated with candles, and dance and song wore away the evening of their last night on board the St. John. The captain dealt out his crew 'a treat of ardent spirits,' and all on board participated in the joys and hopes incident to the termination of their Atlantic passage. Sad, sad finale to their journey.

The following are the names of the few passengers who were saved: - Austin Kearin, Catherine Flanagan, Betsey Higgins, Mary Keane, Michael Fitzpatrick, Michael Gibbon, Barbara Kennelley, Mary Slattery, Michael Cullen, Honor Cullen, Honor Burke, and a Mrs. Quinlan.

## DISASTROUS WRECK AND LOSS OF LIFE

And I quote. "The Boston papers give the following account of a dreadful shipwreck on the Massachusetts coast, during the recent severe gale.

"The British brig, St. John, Captain Oliver, from Galway, Ireland, 5th Ult. For this port, with 120 immigrant passengers, came to anchor wide of Minot Ledge, Cohasset, about six o'clock yesterday morning. She soon, however, dragged her anchor; the masts were then cut away, but continuing to drag, she struck upon the rocks and became a total wreck. The captain, officers, and crew, with the exception of the first mate, took to the boat and landed safely at the Glades, a short distance off; but, as last reported, 'ninety-nine' of the passengers were drowned. There were fourteen cabin passengers, chiefly women and children, who are among the lost. Those who were saved, numbering but 21, got on pieces of the wreck and landed near White Head, at the northern end of the Cohasset Rocks. Twenty-five bodies were washed ashore this evening.

"The names of the drowned are probably unknown to the captain. He reports 126 souls on board, 21 of whom were saved, leaving 99 lost - the brig was in ballast.

"The scene was witnessed from the Glade House, and is represented to have been terrible. The sea ran mountains high, and as soon as she touched, the waves swept the un-fortunate human beings upon her crowded decks by the dozens into the sea. The spectators of this awful sight imagined that they could hear the cries of the victims as they were swept away, but as no boat, save the life-boat, could have lived in the gale, it was impossible to render aid.

"When the St. John struck, her small boat was got ready, but was swamped at the side by a large number jumping into her. Shortly after, the long boat broke her fastening, and floated off from the vessel. The captain and several others swam to, and got on board of her, and landed in safety near Glade House. The second mate, two men and two boys of the crew were drowned.

"After the ship struck the rocks, she thumped, but shortly went to pieces, holding together not more than 50 or 60 minutes. Seven women and three men came ashore on parts of the wreck, alive, but some very much exhausted. Two dead bodies were also taken from pieces of the wreck.

"Great difficulty was experienced in saving those who came ashore, on account of the surf, which would throw them upon the rocks and then carry them to sea again. The poor creatures would cling with a death grip to the clothes of those who came to rescue them, and were, with great difficulty, made to release their hold, even after having reached a place of safety."

*Paul A. Fiori*

The Evening Herald
Boston, Monday October 8, 1849
Third Edition

DREADFUL SHIPWRECK!
LOSS OF ONE HUNDRED AND FORTY FIVE LIVES!

And I quote. "Yesterday forenoon, intelligence was received at the Mariner's Exchange here that two British brigs were seen at anchor off Minot's Ledge, Cohasset, and were in a most perilous situation, owing to the violence of the storm and the probability of their anchors slipping. The steamer R.B. Forbes, as we mentioned in our first edition of this morning, was sent off to the assistance of the two vessels, but was obliged to return in consequence of splitting her mainsail, and because of the terrible violence of the storm, which raged all yesterday and all last night, with little abatement of its fury. The wind was ENE, consequently directly in shore. (The R.B. Forbes would, in less than two years, become the first lightship stationed off Minot Ledge, after the collapse of the 1st Minot Light in the Gale of 1851).

"The fears relative to the above brigs have been dreadfully realized, and the following particulars of the total loss of one of them, and the awful destruction of life consequent on the shipwreck, have been gleaned from Mr. Beal, who runs the Cohasset Express, and other sources of reliable information. It appears that the British brig St. John, Captain Oliver, from Galway (Ireland) with 165 passengers and crew besides, with a cargo of ballast, anchored inside Minot's Ledge about 6 o'clock on Sunday morning (yesterday). There was a dreadful sea on at the time, and the wind blew a perfect hurricane. Such was the violence of the surf, aided by the wind, that the brig dragged her anchors, and was dashed so heavily on the rocks at the point where she lay, as to go to pieces almost immediately...

"From further conversation with the passengers and people of this town, it is certain to our mind that Captain Oliver is liable for ...censure for...his conduct. We would be the last to say one word that would add to the poignancy of his feelings in view of this great disaster; but, in a question involving the lives of more than one hundred fellow beings, we are bound to speak faithfully, the truth, as it has been presented to us.

"It seems that on the afternoon of Saturday 6th inst., he numbered his passengers. Upwards of one hundred names were borne upon the manifest, or list, as two passengers called it who answered the call. A line was then drawn across the deck and between twenty and thirty other names were borne upon a small memorandum book. If the consignee has a duplicate list of passengers, he or they should produce it. Unless a complete list can be produced, we can never fully ascertain the exact number who perished on board this vessel on…October 9 (sic)…

"It is stated by three passengers that, on the afternoon of Saturday, after they had made Cape Cod Light…the Captain mustered his passengers on deck and joyfully assured them that the last night of their confinement on board had arrived… The passage had been a good one…The passengers in the exuberance of their feelings prepared for an illumination; the deck and rigging were decorated with candles and dance and song wore away that evening…The Captain dealt out his crew a "treat of ardent spirits," and all on board participated in the joys and hopes incident to the termination of an Atlantic passage…"

## The Wreck of an Emigrant Ship

And I quote. "The coast of North America was visited by a terrific gale, which caused much disaster among the shipping. An emigrant ship, the St. John, was wrecked near Boston with fearful loss of life. The gale from the northeast commenced on Saturday evening, the 6th of October, and raged with great fury the whole of the night and throughout the day.

"The St. John, Captain Oliver, from Galway, Ireland, anchored inside Minot's Ridge at about 6 o'clock A.M. on Sunday, dragged her anchors and struck on the Grampus rocks about 9 A.M. The captain, officers and crew (with the exception of the 1st mate), took to the boat and landed safe at the Glades. The passengers who were saved got on pieces of the wreck and landed near Whitehead, north end of Cohasset Harbour. The number of passengers on board was about 164, out of which about 145 are supposed to have been lost. There were 14 cabin passengers, mostly women and children.

"Another account states that the brig struck on the rocks known as the Sea Ledges, a little west of Minot Light Ledge, about one mile from shore, and immediately went to pieces. The statements in relation to the number of passengers on board differ. The captain says there were about 114, while the passengers who were saved say there were 150. Of those saved and arrived at Cohasset, 10 in number, 7 were females and 3 males. According to statements of the captain, himself, 8 of the crew and 2 passengers swam to the boat and reached shore in safety; of the others seven men and eight women came ashore on parts of the deck. The total loss of life by his account is 99. All of these came ashore on pieces of the wreck. Two of the women, it is thought, will not survive, one being badly cut on the head by a piece of the wreck. The other woman, whose husband resides in Boston, had 3 children on board with her, all of whom were lost..."

*On Grampus Ledge*

The Boston Evening Journal
October 8, 1849

I found this newspaper article at irelandoldnews.com. I quote it here.

"A severe gale from the NE, commenced on Saturday evening and raged with great fury during the whole of the night and throughout Sunday. Sad, indeed, is the devastation which the gale has wrought upon the coast, and our worst fears are more than realized in the heart rending accounts which we are called upon to chronicle below - and yet we fear that all has not yet been told. Below we give the particulars as we have learned.

"The British brig St. John, Captain Oliver, from Galway, Ireland, anchored inside Minot's Ledge about six o'clock a.m. on Sunday, dragged her anchors and struck the Grampus Rocks about nine a.m. The captain, officers, and crew, with the exception of the 1st mate, took to the [long] boat, and landed safely at the Glades. The passengers who were saved got on pieces of the wreck and landed near Whitehead, north end of Cohasset Harbour. The number of passengers on board was 164, out of which 145 were supposed to have been lost. There were 14 cabin passengers, mostly women and children. Another account states that the captain took to the jolly boat, which swamped and he swam to the long boat and was saved with 10 others, the remainder of the crew were saved.

"Captain Beals of the steamer Mayflower, gives us the following particulars: He understands that the brig struck on the rocks known as the Sea Ledge, a little to the west of Minot's Ledge light about one mile from shore, and immediately went to pieces. There appear to be different statements in relation to the number of passengers on board. The captain says there were but 114, while the passengers who were saved say there were 150. Of those saved and arrived at Cohasset, 10 in number, seven were females and 3 males. Six of them were provided with quarters at the house of Abraham Tower, and the other 4 at Mr. Lathrop's. Two of the women, it is thought, will not survive, one being badly cut on the head by a piece of the wreck. The other woman, it is said, has a husband residing in this city. She had three children on board with her, all of whom were lost. Another gentleman from Cohasset informs us that the brig first went ashore about half-past six o'clock yesterday morning, and shortly after her masts were cut away to ease her. The captain and 10 of the crew then took to the long boat and landed safely near the Glades. Previous to this, however, one of the mates, with 2 of the crew and several of the passengers attempted to leave the brig in the small boat, but she swamped alongside and all were lost. The brig soon drifted on to the Grampus rocks, and almost immediately went to pieces, strewing the beach with fragments. The lifeboat was manned, and every exertion made to save those floating in the surf, on the wreck. Only 10, however, were saved as stated above. Between 20 and 25 of the bodies of those lost had been recovered this morning when our informant left the spot. Preparations were making (sic) by the coroner to have them decently interred. As near as we can ascertain, among the many conflicting stories, there were 21 saved in all – 10 passengers and the captain and 10 of the crew, who came ashore in a long boat. The number lost is impossible to ascertain. According to the captain's story, there were 120 on board including the crew. If this is true, there were 99 lost. The passengers who were saved maintain, however, that there were 150 passengers on board, which, if true, would swell the number to 143!

"The captain and one of the mates, we are informed, arrived in this city from Cohasset on the noon time train, today."

The Boston Journal
145 LIVES LOST!

And I quote. "One of the most disastrous shipwrecks which has occurred on our coast for the last forty years took place at Boston, on Sunday morning, October 7. The British brig St. John, Capt. Oliver of Galway, for Boston, with one hundred and twenty immigrant passengers came to…wide of Minot's Ledge, Cohasset about eight o'clock on Sunday morning. She soon, however, dragged her anchor. The masts were then cut away, but continuing to drag, she struck upon the rocks and became a total wreck. The captain, officers and crew, with the exception of the 1st Mate took to the lifeboat and landed safe at the Glades, a short distance off; but, as last reported ninety-nine of the passengers were drowned. There were fourteen cabin passengers, chiefly women and children, who are among the lost. Those who were saved, numbering but twenty-one, got on pieces of the wreck, and landed near Whitehead, at the north end of the Cohasset Rocks. Twenty-five bodies were washed ashore the next morning.

"The Journal says: The number of passengers onboard was about 164, out of which 145 are supposed to have been lost. There were fourteen cabin passengers, mostly women and children. The Capt. took the jolly boat, which soon swamped, and he swam to the long boast, and was saved with ten others. The 2nd Mate, two men, and two boys were lost. The balance of the crew was saved.

"As near as we can ascertain, among the many confusing stories, there were 21 saved in all – 10 passengers, the captain, and 10 of the crew, who came ashore in the long boat. The number lost is impossible to ascertain. According to the captain's story, there were 120 on board, including the crew. If this is true, there are but 99 lost. The passengers who were saved maintain, however, that there were 150 passengers on board, which, if true, would swell the number lost to 143! The former account is probably the true one.

"Of those saved and arrived at Cohasset, 10 in number, seven were females and three were males. All these came ashore on pieces of the wreck. Two of the women, it is thought, will not survive – one being badly cut on the head by a piece of the wreck. The other woman, it is said, has a husband residing in the city. She had three children on board with her, all of whom were lost.

"The shipping in Boston Harbor suffered Considerably during Saturday night, but no serious damage is recorded. In all the eastern ports the gale was severely felt. A number of brigs and schooners are reported by the Boston papers to have got ashore off Cohasset Bay, but there had been no loss of life, and it was expected they would get off. Some anxiety is felt for the packet-ship Washington Irving, which left Boston on Saturday for Liverpool, but from the report of a captain arrived, it is thought she succeeded in clearing Cape Cod, and getting to sea."

The Boston Post
October 9, 1849

And I quote. "...British brig seen at anchor inside Minot's Light during the storm of Sunday morning, dragged her anchors, struck on Grampus Rocks and went to pieces before 9 a.m. She proved to be the brig St. John, Captain Oliver, from Galway, Ireland, with emigrants. Of these it seems fully 99 perished; Captain Oliver and his surviving mate reached town on Monday, and the Captain gave the following account:

"Saturday, 5 p.m.: passed Cape Cod with a light NE wind, weather thick, hove to with a head to...At 4 a.m. wore ship, wind S, made Minot's Ledge. Not having to wear ship, ventured to run where we saw a ship inside of the ledge. The violence of the gale and heavy seas caused us to drag our anchors, when we cut away our masts and held on but a short time before she broke up.

"Previous to breaking up the jolly boat was hanging by the tackles alongside when the stern ring bolt broke and she fell into the water. The captain, 2nd mate and two boys got into her to clear her when about 25 passengers jumped into her and swamped her; the passengers together with the 2nd mate and two boys perished. The captain caught a rope hanging over the quarter, and was drawn on board by the 1st mate.

"The long boat was got clear shortly after, and a heavy sea coming on board carried her from the vessel, when a number of passengers jumped over to swim to her, but all perished, the captain, 1st mate (Mr. Cummerford), 8 of the crew and 2 passengers swam to the boat and reached the shore in safety. Ten others, 7 men and 3 women, came ashore on part of the deck. Total loss of life: 99; saved: 22; 25 of the dead have washed ashore this morning.

"Passengers saved: Austin Kearn, Catherine Flanagan, Betsey Higgins, Mary Cane, Michael Fitzpatrick, Michael Gibbon, Barbara Kennelly, Mary Slattery, Michael Redding, Honora Cullen, Honora Burke. The names of the 99 lost cannot be obtained. Up to 4 o'clock on Monday afternoon, 27 bodies had been washed ashore: 21 men, 3 women and 3 children. They will be buried today. The citizens of

Cohasset are doing everything in their power to render the condition of the survivors as comfortable as possible; and every exertion is made to secure the bodies of those who have perished.

"The striking of the vessel was seen from the public house at the Glades, and the poor unfortunates were swept from her decks by the hungry waves while the spectators had no power to aid them. In sixty minutes the wreck was thumped into fragments. A portion of the passengers, women and children, being below, perished there. During the day, the shore was lined with spectators, who did what they could to save the bodies washed upon the beach. Great difficulty was experienced in saving those who came ashore on pieces of the wreck, on account of the surf, which would throw them upon the rocks and then carry them to sea again. Of seven first class passengers, who were all lost, were three girls, the nieces of the owner of the vessel.

"The other brig which was seen at anchor near where the St. John went ashore, was the British brig Kathleen, Captain Barnaby, from Pictou to Boston, with coal. The lifeboat went to her assistance and she rode out the gale in safety.

"The steam tug, R.B. Forbes, went below again on Monday morning as far as Cohasset but found no wrecks."

The Boston Daily Bee
October 9, 1849

DISASTER BY THE LATE STORM
AWFUL SHIPWRECK AT MINOT"S LEDGE
ABOUT 100 DROWNED – MEN, WOMEN, AND CHILDREN

I found this article at wreckhunter.net and quote it here.

"Br. brig St. John, Capt. Oliver, from Galway (Ireland), Sept. 5th, anchored inside of Minot's Ledge, Saturday night. At about 7 A.M., on Sunday morning, she dragged her anchors and struck the rocks. The following particulars of her loss, together with that of 99 of her passengers and crew, is gleaned from various persons who witnessed the disaster.

"The vessel struck at about 7 A.M. yesterday. The scene was witnessed from the Glades House, and is represented to have been terrible. The sea ran mountains high, and as soon as she touched, the waves swept the unfortunate human beings upon her crowded decks by the dozens into the sea. The spectators of this awful sight imagined they could hear the cries of the victims as they were swept away, but as no boat, save the life-boat, could have lived in the gale, it was found impossible to render aid.

"The life-boat left Cohasset early in the morning, and went to the aid of the British brig which was in danger at the mouth of the harbor, and carried her to a place of safety, they did not, however, visit the wreck, supposing that the long boat which they met going towards the shore, contained all that belonged to her.

"When the St. John struck, her small boat was got ready, but was swamped at the side by a large number jumping into her. Shortly after, the long boat broke her fastening, and floated off from the vessel. The Captain and several others swam to and got on board of her, and landed in safety near the Glades House. The second mate, 2 men and 2 boys of the crew were drowned.

"After the ship struck the rocks, she thumped awhile, but shortly went to pieces, holding together not more than 50 or 60 minutes.

Paul A. Fiori

Seven women and three men came ashore on pieces of the wreck, alive, but some very exhausted. Two dead bodies were also taken from pieces of the wreck.

"Early in the forenoon, the news of the wreck began to spread, and in the afternoon, the shore was lined with people, who were active in getting bodies from the surf. Mr. Holmes, a railroad conductor, was busy during the entire day in aiding the living and removing the dead bodies from the waves. One man, whose name we did not learn, came near losing his life in rescuing a body from the surf.

"Towards nightfall, the bodies began to come ashore, and quite a number were taken from the surf, all however, dead. Dead bodies would be thrown upon the rocks, but before they could be recovered, the sea would carry them back again.

"Quite a number of passengers, especially women and children, were below when she struck, and were probably drowned there, as a hole was almost immediately thumped in her bottom. The long boat that reached the shore in safety contained, in addition to the captain and crew, one passenger. Of 7 first class passengers, who were all lost, were 3 girls, nieces of the owner of the vessel. Great difficulty was experienced in saving those who came ashore on pieces of the wreck, on account of the surf, which would throw them upon the rocks and then carry them to sea again. The poor creatures would cling with a death-like grip to the clothes of those who came to rescue them, and were, with difficulty, made to release their hold, even after having reached a place of safety. One woman saved was very badly bruised upon the rocks, and it was thought, last night, that she would die, but she is this morning, more comfortable.

"It is stated that one passenger, clinging to a piece of the wreck, floated to the rocks, but was so far gone as to be unable to unclench his hand. Finally, someone jumped on the fragment, made fast a rope to him, and he was got ashore. His face of a deep purple, his open mouth, fixed teeth, and deathly eyes, formed a sight long to be remembered.

"So far, only twenty-five bodies have been recovered, but the surf, which yet runs very high, is full of them. Before nightfall, many more will doubtless be taken out. The shore is strewn with the baggage of the passengers, all stove to pieces.

"Capt. Oliver and his surviving mate reached this city at 12 o'clock... The names of the drowned are probably unknown to the captain. He reports 120 souls on board, 21 of whom were saved, leaving 99 lost. The following named persons were saved: Austin Kearin, Katherine Flannagan, Betsey Higgins, Mary Kane, Michael Fitzpatrick, Michael Gibbon, Barbara Kennelly, Mary Slattery, Michael Redding, Honora Cullen, and Honora Burke.

"Twenty-seven bodies have come ashore, up to 4 o'clock, P.M., yesterday, 21 females, 3 males, and 3 children."

The Boston Transcript
October 9, 1849
THE WRECK OF THE BRIG ST. JOHN

And I quote. "There seems to be some discrepancy in the statements as to the number on board the ill-fated St. John. Captain Oliver reports the whole number as 120, while passengers saved and some of the crew, it is stated, asserts that the number was at least 150. It is certain, however, that but eleven passengers were saved, together with the captain and most of the crew, numbering ten more - 21 in all. The second mate, two men and two boys, were lost…the citizens of Cohasset are doing every thing in their power to render the condition of the survivors as comfortable as possible. Up to 4 o'clock yesterday afternoon 27 bodies had been washed ashore- 21 women, 3 men, and 3 children. They will be interred today."

The Boston Post
October 10, 1849
THE ST. JOHN SHIPWRECK

And I quote. "There is no reason to doubt the captain's statement that she had 120 souls on board when she struck Minot's Ledge. The names of the passengers in the cabin were three Misses Flannagan's, two Misses Slattery's, Bridget Quinn, and Eliza O'Brien, with several children. They were all lost. The Flannagan's were the nieces of the owner. The following are some of the names of the lost: - Michael Cormaine, Michael Flanagan, John Batton, John Dolan and his wife, John and James Laheff, Nappy and Thomas Farlye, Bridget Madigan, a Miss Brooks, Honora Mullen, Honora Quinlan, and Mrs. Cornelia. Margaret Ronan, Catharine Henif, Mary Henif, Peggy Mullen, Mary Curtain, Bridget Kane, Catharine Swaney, and Mary Freeman. Patrick Swaney, whose body was recovered, lost eleven children, washed from the wreck by the same wave that carried him into the surge. Names of some whose bodies were recovered: - Mary Freeman, Mary Joice and a child, Patrick Swaney and eleven children, also his servant girl, Martha Fahey. John Dolan and his wife, Sally Swaney, Peggy Fahey and a child unknown, Mary Freeman, Catherine Fitzpatrick, Peggy Miller and her sister's child, Bridget Burke, John Laheff, a female, and five persons unknown.

"Among those lost were Bridgett Kennelly, wife of Patrick Kennelly of this city; Honora Donnelly, 16, who has a sister in Lynn; Honora, Mary, and Margaret Mulkennan, children of Mrs. Mulkennan of 4th Street, South Boston; one woman with 11 children who has a husband in Massachusetts; Honora and Thomas Lahey; two sisters of Mrs. McDermott of Springfield."

*Paul A. Fiori*

The Boston Daily Herald
October 10, 1849
FUNERAL
THE BURIAL OF THE VICTIMS OF THE ST. JOHN
A MELANCHOLY SIGHT

The following newspaper article was found on "clarelibrary.ie" www.clarelibrary.ie, as were the articles from The Burlington Hawkeye, and The Alton Telegraph and Democratic Review, and they are reprinted here, and I quote.

"One of our reporters visited the scene of the lamentable catastrophe yesterday, and states that the sight was heart-rending in the extreme. The shore, for about a mile in length, was strewed with portions of the wreck. Some of the bodies were shockingly mutilated. The forehead of one woman was horribly mangled, the flesh from the right leg of another was torn from above the knee to the feet; all the others were more or less bruised; with the exception of one young girl, recognized as Sally Sweeney, whose person exhibited no injuries. Her features were as calm and placid as if she were enjoying a quiet and pleasant slumber. It was expected that the tide would float in more.

"An inquest was held, and a verdict rendered in accordance with the facts heretofore given…

"After remaining on the beach until 11 o'clock, the lids of the coffins were nailed down, and the bodies were then removed in wagons to the church. Here religious ceremonies were performed by the Rev. Messrs. Osgood and Reed of Cohasset, and after at the grave by Rev. Mr. Redden a Catholic Clergyman from Quincy.

"The bodies are all buried in one grave, which was some 20' long, by 9' broad, and 6' in depth.

"An interesting incident occurred as the coffins were being placed under the final covering. The cars from Boston arrived at that moment, and among the passengers were the sisters of Peggy Adams, one of the victims, and her husband, from South Boston. At the inquest, the coffin was opened and a most melancholy scene ensued. The sister's agony was most poignant, and exhibited itself in such a manner as to touch all hearts. What a melancholy meeting after so many days of joyful anticipation.

"Too much praise cannot be awarded to the generous-hearted citizens of Cohasset – male and female – for their noble conduct of the whole affair. One of them, Mr. Charles Studley, nearly lost his life in attempting to rescue the living and secure the bodies of the dead. Dr. Foster, an able physician of the town, also deserves praise for his unremitting exertions on behalf of the survivors."

*Paul A. Fiori*

The Burlington Hawkeye
Burlington, Iowa
October 25, 1849

DERADFUL SHIPWRECK
LOSS OF ONE HUNDRED AND FIFTY LIVES

And I quote. "New York, October 1849 – We learn from Boston that the brig St. John, from Galway, Ireland, for Boston, struck against the Grampus Rocks on Sunday morning last, at about 9 o'clock, and sank almost instantly, having been in pieces. By this painful calamity, it is estimated that about One hundred and fifty passengers were saved by floating on pieces of the wreck. Twenty-five of the dead bodies were washed ashore and picked up Monday morning. The captain thinks that the loss of life is not so great, but others saved believe it cannot be less than stated above."

Alton Telegraph and Democratic Review
Alton, Illinois
October 26, 1849

And I quote. "It is stated that the British brig St. John, from Galway, Ireland, and bound for Boston, struck against the Grampus Rocks, on the morning of the 30th ult., and sank almost immediately, having gone to pieces. The captain, crew, and ten of the passengers, saved themselves, with difficulty, on fragments of the wreck; but the remainder, about 100 souls, found a watery grave."

*Paul A. Fiori*

The Cohasset Town Records: Vital Records
Book Two- Births And Deaths 1844-1862
Report Written By Newcomb Bates, Jr., Town Clerk.

And I quote. "On the seventh of October, the brig St. John, from Ireland, was lost on our rocks, by which casualty- about 100 persons, male and female, old and young (mostly young) lost their lives. The following out of fifty bodies which have been recovered and buried in our Burying Ground, have been recognized by the five survivors: Catharine Fitzgerald, Peggy Mullen and her sisters child, Bridget Mulligaw, Bridget Burke, Peggy Purky, Sally Sweeney, John Dolan and his wife, Martha Perky, Patrick Sweeney, ---Lahiffs (a female), Mary Freeman, Mary Joice. The funeral of the first twenty- five was held in the Unitarian Meeting House, on Tuesday afternoon following the wreck, when a crowded audience attended and services were performed by the Rev. Mr. Osgood and Rev. Mr. Reed of the Orthodox Society. After which the procession walked to the grave, where further ceremonies were gone through by Mr. Rodden, Roman Catholic Priest of Quincy. For further particulars, see newspapers on file at the Clerk's Office."

## On Grampus Ledge

The Wreck of the Immigrant Brig St. John
Statement of the exertions made by the Life Boats at Cohasset and their crews in endeavoring to save the people while they were in a very dangerous situation within
The Cohasset Rocks on the 7th of October, 1849.

And I quote. "It was 6 1/2 A.M. on Sunday morning, October 7, 1849, during a very severe storm, with wind from North East, that two Brigs were discovered at anchor among the Rocks and Breakers. One of these, which proved to be the (British Brig) St. John, was lying in the breakers between the Grampuses and Sea Ledges, about two miles from the entrance of Cohasset harbor where the Life Boats are stationed. (The other Brig was the Kathleen.)

"From that point the distressed brigs could not be very distinctly seen, but the opinion of those present was that one, the St. John was in a very dangerous situation. If she should strike the bottom, all hands would be lost. She was completely surrounded by heavy Breakers and it was very doubtful whether a Life Boat could pull out against the tremendous Sea and Gale that prevailed at the time. If they succeeded in pulling out over the Breakers over the Bar which would have taken two hours at least, they (the Life Boat) could not have come near enough to render any assistance as the vessel was completely enveloped in Breakers." (The time of high tide is not mentioned.)

"At about 7 ½ o'clock, (AM) it was discovered that the St. John had cut away her masts. Then the conclusion was that she would hold on by her anchors and that a powerful steam boat like the R.B. Forbes, by getting to windward of her, could put over a buoy and by that means at a favorable time take her from her perilous situation.

"This appeared to be the only chance of saving the crew. An express went immediately to Boston, but on arrival they found that the R.B. Forbes had proceeded for the vessels.

"The people of Cohasset got the two Life Boats ready (at Whitehead) as fast as possible. About 8 o'clock they began to pull out for the wrecks. The Largest Boat with nine men was able to pull ahead but very slowly against the tremendous Sea and Wind.

"Shipping much water they directed their course for the wreck St. John among the Breakers. After pulling about ¾ of an hour they discovered there was very little to be seen of her.

"About this time her long boat was discovered to windward and as near as they could judge had 11 men in her. Supposing her (the St. John) to be a vessel of about 200 tons they were well convinced that this was all their crew and that they would land safe, as the wind and sea were favorable. They (the life boat people) were more fully confirmed in the opinion that this was all the crew as the Boat did not show any intention of communicating with us which they might easily have done being directly to Windward of us." (Bigelow's account states this longboat with the captain, first mate; eight of the crew and two passengers reached shore at the Glades.)

"The other Brig, (the Kathleen) at this time, having her colors at half Mast, Union down, was supposed to be sinking. They concluded to pull and reach her if possible. After very hard pulling they succeeded in getting along Side. She had not struck the bottom at this time, it being about 11 ½ A.M. The Captain wished them to take his passengers out, as he feared if the Gale continued she would drift in among the Breakers, and they would be lost. Five children were thrown into the Boat. In doing so the Boat struck the Side and injured some. They directed the captain how to steer if they struck a Drift, to keep safe. She struck a drift soon after, the Captain followed their instructions and got on to the flats where she now lays safe. She struck on the Bar and lost her Rudder.

"The Crews of the Boats lifeboats on landing were much astonished to find that the St. John had immigrants in and that there were many lives lost. They could easier have got into the vicinity of this wreck and have picked up those hanging to the wreck stuff clear of the Breakers if they had known there were any more on board.

"That would have been rather than to have proceeded to the other Brig further to windward which they supposed could not be in imminent danger of going to pieces.

"The St. John, where she broke up, so far from the shore, on a very large ledge, the Sea breaking very high, a large space around her, so that it would have been impossible for a Boat to have got near her from the Lee ward. Therefore any one having any experience in disasters of this kind must know if She Broke up in such a Gale as that in such a situation there must inevitably be a large proportion of them Lost from so large a number.

"The Small Life Boat with 7 men in pulled for some time against Sea and Wind until the crew became exhausted as they made but little or no progress. Since it would be impossible to get her and to the place of the disaster they were obliged to return.

"As this disaster as to loss of Life has been the Greatest that has ever happened near this place we make this statement of the exertions made by the Crews of the Life Boats. Having been requested to give an account of the Services Rendered in these cases by the Life Boats and this disaster as to loss of life is the Greatest that has happened near this place.

"(The above statement bears no date, but presumably was written fairly soon after Oct. 7, 1849 by Captain Lothrop while the experience was fresh in his mind. In places the account seems to be written first hand but he does not indicate definitely that he was in one of the lifeboats. This statement was written after Daniel T. Lothrop wrote his letter of April 15, 1847, addressed to Captain W.H. Swift which listed the vessels wrecked near Minot's Ledge as quoted on Page 461-62 of Narrative History.)"

*Paul A. Fiori*

Miss Lucy Treat has a diary written by a Miss Elizabeth Lothrop who observed the breaking up of the wreck from the Lothrop house at Sandy Cove and recorded what she saw. And I quote.

"The St. John Sinking: Tuesday Oct. 7, 1849

"I arrived home a week ago last Tuesday and I have had such unpleasant weather I have not had an opportunity to look about me. Then last Sunday my eyes were opened in the following manner: about eight o'clock I made a visit to the…room for something, where I heard an exclamation from one of the boys, which drew my attention on the sea, where I saw two brigs, one anchored in the midst of the rocks with the sea breaking upon her from all sides, the other farther off and apparently out of danger. I went below and informed father, he looked out and said, "There is difficulty there." Soon her masts were cut away. Father had gone to join the life boat, my brothers all for the beach, I noticed she drifted in rapidly, and if her anchors could not hold her she would inevitably soon be on the rocks where the waves were fast forcing her with horrible vengeance, no human power could stay those waves, their aim was destruction, and how forcibly it was carried into execution was soon declared to my horror stricken vision. In about an hour after her masts were cut away nothing was visible, in a moment she had gone to atoms and the sea had washed over the fragments, freighted with human beings. Soon, portions of the brig could be seen making for shore now towering up mountains high and then sinking into the depths of hell. Whether there were human beings on board the wreck for the thickness of the storm prevented me from determining then.

"Soon the multitudes with which the beach was thronged began to wave their hats and halloo, and I understood afterwards that when they observed people on the wreck, it was a motion for a whale boat to come alongside, which paid no heed to the demand, which was one of the many inhuman actions of the day, which displayed such perfect indifference to human suffering, such unaccountable hardness of heart that thinks of nothing but self ease and protection. The waving of hats led me to infer there were human beings on board the wreck. I forthwith began to put things in readiness heat rooms and blanket made beds, as ours is the nearest house the sufferers would all be brought in for relief. I had enough to do, with an occasional glance out the window when at last I perceived some miserable looking creatures, that reminded me of drowned rats approaching they could scarcely walk and were led by men on either side of them, our doors were open to receive them. Such a shuddering shivering my ears never heard before, and such a set of half-drowned half-naked frightened creatures my eyes never beheld.

"Three men were first brought in and then a lot of women, all Irish. What conclusion to make I did not if it were not for the exigency of the moment; we should have been over powered by excitement. We placed them in bed, and used every exertion to restore animation to two of the women whose moans could be heard through the house. These two were senseless when taken from the wreck; towards night, six were able to go to the village in a week the worst were conveyed to the poor house."

I attended church today after a long absence, but my mind is so full of everything, I cannot pay much attention to the discourses. A dancing school has commenced I do not attend it but my mind runs that way; then this horrible shipwreck, and to the continual picking up of dead bodies on our beach, has so excited my mind that I tell them I shall never get over it.

"I took a walk on the beach after meeting, and there I saw two or three dead bodies stretched out. I did not approach very near to them as I was told; they looked like anything but human beings. Last Wednesday I called at the poor house to see those two that were taken from here a day or two previous. Mrs. Quinlan and Mrs. Burke, I found they had improved rapidly. I should judge they had good care taken of them. I found but twelve paupers in the poor house, and some are curious looking objects…"

Elizabeth Lothrop
Age 19,
Diary of Tuesday, October 11- Wednesday, October 25, 1849.

"P. S....Some time ago I received a note, including $10, from the L.T. Society of this place, for kindness to the St. John survivors, yesterday it was returned, thinking it might be better employed."

BRIG ST. JOHN FROM GALWAY, IRELAND
LOST OCTOBER 7, 1849
OFF COHASSET
By Representative Michael Flaherty
(Undated)

And I quote. "In the December 11, 1988 edition of the South Boston Tribune, I made reference to a tragic shipwreck with the loss of ninety-nine Irish men, women, and children. This wreck took place on Grampus Ledge off Cohasset, on Sunday morning, October 7, 1849. The ship was the British Brig St. John from Galway, Ireland. The St. John was loaded with immigrants from County Galway and County Clare who had sailed from their famine-stricken land no doubt in hopes of finding a better way of life in America. The occasion for my making reference to the sinking of the St. John at that time with its terrible loss of Irish lives was when I was presented a charter to the officers of the newly organized Boston Gaelic Fire Brigade. The presentation ceremony [was] held in my office at the State House. I had been requested by the officers of the Brigade, who are members of the Boston Fire Department, to assist them with their by-laws and constitution. At the conclusion of the ceremony, I mentioned to the officers of the Brigade, that among its goals was to encourage its membership to improve themselves in, to promote, the study of the research into Irish Civilisation, with special emphasis upon the inter-relationship between Gaelic and American cultures. I spoke of the tragic shipwreck which took place off Cohasset not too far from Boston, and I suggested to the officers of the Brigade that perhaps they might care to visit and decorate this final resting place of those poor souls from County Galway and County Clare who almost made it to America. The gravesite is marked with a huge granite Celtic Cross that overlooks Cohasset Harbor, from perhaps the highest point in the Cohasset Central Cemetery (Author's Note: The Cross actually overlooks Little Harbor, Sandy Beach, and the Atlantic Ocean. The harbor is about a mile away, and cannot be seen from any point near the Cross).

"The Ancient Order of Hibernians would annually make a pilgrimage to the cemetery and decorate the gravesite. Memorial Day,

*Paul A. Fiori*

1984, will mark the seventieth year since this monument was erected. It would be fitting if a prayer was said or perhaps a flower left at the base of this monument by people of Irish heritage, especially those from the west of Ireland, County Galway, or County Clare. My interest in this particular event in Irish history in America, is because I recall the shipwreck and the grave in Cohasset as being discussed by both my parents and my grandparents in my home.

Since my reporting this tragic event last December in the South Boston Tribune, I have received numerous inquiries seeking additional information surrounding the wreck, pictures of the grave, and especially the names of the passengers on the St. John and their homes in Ireland. I have obtained a list of the crew and the passengers who sailed from Galway on the St. John, and the list gives the names of those who were lost and saved. The list was printed in the Boston Post, October 12, 1849. I believe some of the homes may be spelled wrong. Perhaps Innistival, Co. Clare, should be Ennistymon and Innes, County Clare, may be Ennis, County Clare.

# THE SHIPWRECK OF THE ST. JOHN
(Ennistymon Parish Magazine)
(1996)

And I quote. "One of the most tragic events to occur during the mass exodus from Ireland in the aftermath of the Great Famine was the shipwreck of St. John and the loss of nearly 100 lives, many of whom were from Ennistymon, Lahinch, and Kilfenora, off the coast of Massachusetts in October 1849.

"On 7 September 1849, the St. John, a brig of about 200 tons, sailed out of Galway bound for Boston. She was owned by Henry Comerford of Galway and Ballykeale House, Kilfenora; and Captain Oliver from Bohermore, Galway, was in command. Aboard were nine crewmembers and about one hundred passengers from North Clare and Connemara. On Saturday, 6th October the ship came close to land near Cape Cod almost at the end of her journey to Massachusetts Bay. They voyage had been a good one and the captain had a ration of grog issued to the crew and he suggested to the passengers that they might celebrate their last night aboard the St. John. They, too, had every reason for merriment; they had left far behind them a country of starvation, disease, and death, the voyage had been less of a trial than they had expected and they were on the shores of the golden land. They hurried to decorate the rigging and decks with candles, and 'passed the night in song and dance.'

"At five o'clock in the evening they passed Cape Cod Light and were off Scituate Light at one o'clock in the morning. But, already the ship was being driven towards the shore by a fierce north-easterly gale. The captain stood to the northwards to clear the land until daylight, which would normally have come at about quarter to six. By then the gale had become a full storm and the ship was being driven southwards along the Massachusetts coast and was by morning at the mouth of Cohasset Bay. The captain described the weather as 'very thick'; the people who crowded the shore said that the waves 'were mountains high'. Inexorably the wind drove the little ship towards the shore. The brig came inside Minot's Lighthouse and the Captain tried to 'wear away' up to another brig which was lying at anchor just inside the breakers at Hocksett Rock, but the sails were in shreds and the storm too powerful. Both anchors were dropped, but they dragged. As a last resort Captain Oliver had both masts cut away but the wind and seas were relentless, and the brig was driven onto Grampus Ledge. It was the seven o'clock on Sunday morning.

"Enormous waves lifted the helpless ship and smashed her again and again on the rocks. The impact broke her back and opened her seams. A hole was quickly broken in her hull and those below decks were drowned within minutes. Pounded against the rocks, the brig began to break up. Horrified spectators saw people being 'swept in their dozens' into the boiling surf from the crowded decks. Even though they were deafened by the howling wind and the thunder of the seas, the watchers were convinced that they could hear the screams of the unfortunates as they were swept to their deaths.

### THE SHIP WAS QUICKLY DISINTEGRATING…

"The jollyboat was hanging by its tackle alongside. The stern rigging bolt broke, the boat fell into the water and was being swept away. The captain, the second mate, two of the crewmen and two apprentice boys jumped into the maelstrom to secure her but about twenty-five frenzied passengers attempted to board the boat and it was swamped. Of the people in or around the jollyboat, only one survived; Captain Oliver grabbed a rope which was hanging from the quarter and was pulled aboard the ship by the first mate, Henry Comerford (believed to be a nephew of the ship's owner of the same name).

"When the long boat was got clear, a number of passengers jumped into the water to reach her, but all perished. By now, the ship was quickly disintegrating and the water around her was strewn with wreckage to which people clung desperately even though they were again and again buried beneath tons of water as the colossal waves broke over them. The captain, the first mate and the remaining seven members of the crew succeeded in reaching the longboat, but only one passenger. As they made their way to shore, they met with the lifeboat coming out of Cohasset to the aid of another emigrant ship, Kathleen, which was in difficulties at the mouth of the harbour. Blinded by the flying spray and spume, and deafened by the waves and wind, the crew of the lifeboat had no inkling of the tragedy so close to them; they assumed that the longboat contained the entire complement of the brig and continued on their mission to assist the Kathleen.

"By eight a.m. the ship had completely broken up and the worst horror was over. Eight women and four men had made their way to the shore, almost dead of exhaustion. Some had to have hands prised from the wreckage, which had saved their lives. News of the disaster had spread and by early afternoon the shore was lined with people who worked unsparingly to rescue the living and retrieve the dead. They had many stories to tell. Two of the women who had fought their way to shore had each lost three children. Patrick Sweeney of Galway had perished with his wife and nine children. Many of the bodies were badly mutilated by the jagged rocks, yet Sally Sweeney's 'features were calm and placid, as if she were enjoying a quiet and pleasant slumber.' Mr. Lathrop, in whose house the survivors found shelter, waded into the surf to retrieve a parcel of clothing and found that he had an infant in his arms; some days later the baby was said to be in excelent health.

"Time and again the bodies were thrown on the rocks by the breakers, only to be swept again into deep water by the backwash. Charles Studley was so determined to bring one such body to shore that it was only with great difficulty that he himself was rescued.

"The American writer, Henry David Thoreau was in Boston when the tragedy occurred and made his way to Cohasset where he met 'several hay-riggings and farm-wagons each loaded with three large, rough deal boxes. We do not need to ask what was in them. The owners of the wagons were made the undertakers. Many horses in carriages were fastened to the fences near the shore, and for a mile or more, up and down, the beach was covered with people looking out for bodies, and examining the fragments of the wreck. It was now Tuesday morning and the sea was still breaking violently on the rocks. There were eighteen or twenty of the same large boxes I have mentioned lying on a green hillside and surrounded by a crowd. The bodies which had been recovered, twenty seven or eight in all, had been collected there.'

"Thoreau further relates that a woman who had immigrated from Ireland in an earlier ship 'but had left her infant behind for her sister to bring, came and looked into these boxes, and saw in one her child in her sister's arms, sas if the sister had meant to be found thus; and within three days after, the mother died from the effect of the sight.'

## FORTY-SIX BODIES HAD BEEN TAKEN FROM THE SEA…

"A newspaper report of the time says that forty-six bodies had been taken from the sea by nightfall, that they were coffined on the beach and, after religious ceremonies on the beach and in the cemetery, were buried in a common grave on Tuesday. Thoreau describes seeing the funeral headed by the captain and the survivors. He ruminates that 'on the whole, it was not so impressive a scene as I might have expected. The sight of one body affects us deeply but the sight of so many bodies blunted the sensibilities.'

"Sixty-five years later a huge granite Celtic Cross was raised over the grave, sited on the highest point of Cohasset Central Cemetery so as to command a view of the bay. The cross bears the inscription: 'This Cross Was Erected And Dedicated May 30, 1914, By The A.O.H. And The I.A.A.O.H. Of Massachusetts To Mark The Final Resting Place Of About Forty-Five Irish Immigrants From A Total Company Of Ninety-Nine Who Lost Their Lives On Grampus Ledge Off Cohasset, October 7, 1849, In The Wreck Of The Brig St. John From Galway, Ireland. R.I.P.'"

# *APPENDIX B*
## *Passenger Lists and Confusion*

The passenger lists shown below are partial or complete lists, depending on the source used. Since any real list was lost during the wreck, I have had to rely on the sources available to me. The lists are full of misspellings, of both passenger names and towns they originated from. Any corrections will take place at the end of this chapter.

It seems that after leaving Galway Harbor, Captain Oliver, perhaps at Henry Comerford's request, stopped at Lettermullen. Before leaving Galway, Oliver had entered the names of one hundred eleven passengers on the ship's manifest. At Lettermullen another fifty three passengers boarded the St. John. There were now one hundred and sixty four passengers on the ship.

Passengers Saved – (taken from The Galway Vindicator) – Austin Kearin, Catherine Flanagan, Betsy Higgins, Mary Keane, Michael Fitzpatrick, Michael Gibbon, Barbara Kennelly, Mary Slattery, Michael Redding, Honor Cullen, Honor Burke, and Mrs. Quinlan.

Passengers saved – (taken from The Boston Evening Journal. Oct. 8, 1849) – Austin Kearn, Catherine Flanagan, Betsey Higgins, Mary Keane, Michael Fitzpatrick, Michael Gibbon, Barbara Kennelly, Mary Slattery, Michael Redding, Honora Cullen, and Honora Burke.

Passengers Saved – (taken from The Boston Transcript. Oct. 9, 1849) – Austin Kearn, Catharine Flanagan, Betsey Higgins, Mary

Cane, Michael Fitzpatrick, Michael Gibbon, Barbara Kennelly, Mary Slattery, Michael Redding, Honora Cullen, and Honora Burke.

Cabin Passengers Lost – (taken from The Boston Post. Oct. 10, 1849) – Three Misses Flannagan's, two Misses Slattery's, Bridget Quinn, and Eliza O'Brien.

Steerage Passengers Lost – (taken from The Boston Post. Oct. 10, 1849) – Michael Comaine, Michael Flanagan, John Batton, John Dolan and his wife, John and James Loheff, Nappy and Thomas Farlye, Bridget Madigan, Miss Brooks, Honora Mullen, Honora Quinlan and Mrs. Cornelia, Margaret Kanan, Catharine Henif, Mary Henif, Peggy Mullen, Mary Curtain, Bridget Kane, Catharine Swaney and Mary Freeman, Patrick Swaney and his eleven children, Mary Joice and her child, a servant girl, Martha Fahey, Peggy Fahey and a child not known, Catharine Fitzpatrick, Peggy Miller and her sister's child, Bridget Burke, a female, and six persons unknown. Also, Bridget Kennelly and her three children, she is the wife of Patrick Kennelly of Boston, Honora Donnelly, 16, who has a sister in Lynn, Honora, Mary, and Margaret Mulkennan, children of Mrs. Mulkennan of 4th Street, South Boston, one woman with eleven children who has a husband in Massachusetts, Honora and Thomas Lahey, and two sisters of Mrs. McDermott of Springfield.

Passengers Saved – (taken from The Boston Post. Oct. 12, 1849) – Austin Kearin (20),
Betsy Higgins (21), Michael Fitzpatrick (26), Barbara Kennelly (20), Michael Redding (24), Mary or Honor Burke (27; lost three children), Catherine Flanagan (20), Mary Kane (24), Michael Gibbon (26), Mary Slattery (20), Honora Cullen (28; lost three children).

Crew Saved – (taken from The Boston Post. Oct. 12, 1849) – Captain Oliver, 1st Mate Henry Cummerford, Henry O'Hern, Michael Kennelly, William Larkin, Isaac Cummerford, Thomas Walker, James Flaherty, and Andrew Frost.

Crew Lost – (taken from The Boston Post. Oct. 12, 1849) – Antonio McDonough, William Thompson, Michael Conners, William Angiers, Edward Kennelly, and two apprentice boys.

Cabin Passengers Lost – (taken from The Boston Post. Oct. 12, 1849) – of Kilnare, Co. Clare: Mary, Nancy, and Margaret Hannagan.
Of Innistivan, Co. Clare: Bridget Quinn and Eliza O'Brien.

Steerage Passengers Lost – (taken from The Boston Post. Oct. 12, 1849) – of Inistivan, Co. Clare: Ann Slattery, Bridget Slattery, Hugh Madigan, and Margaret Keenan.
Of Innistivan, Co. Clare: Hugh Glynn.
Of Issistivan, Co. Clare: Margaret Keenan and a Miss Brooks.
Of Lalinen, Co. Clare: Michael Hannagan.
Of Killanara, Co. Clare: Patrick Lahiff, John Lahiff, Thomas Riley, and Bridget Maddigan.
Of Roan, Co. Clare: Bridget McMahan, Patrick McMahan, Catherine McMahan, Mary Nalon, and Mary Frowley and child.
Of Innes, Co. Clare: Mary Freeman and child, Mr. Egan, his wife, and daughter.
Of Dyant, Co. Clare: Martin Sexton, Jeremiah Murphy, and James Moran.
Of Anch, Co. Clare: Daniel Byrnes, Michael Griffen, Catherine Burnes, Peggy Molloy, and Ellen Hasset.
Of Kilmary, Co. Clare: Patrick McGrath, James McGrath, Winny Galvin, Mary Galvin, Margaret Kane, and Mary McNamara.
Of Clare, Co. Clare: Honora Lahiff, or Rohan, John Lahiff, or Rohan, Mary Curtis, Honora Mulkenan, Mary Mulkenan, and Margaret Mulkenan.
Of Kunnanmar, Co. Galway: Bridget Connelly, Patrick Sweeny, his wife, and nine children.
Of Galway, Co. Galway: Patrick Corman, Miles Sweeney, Thomas Burke, Eliza Burke, Mary McDermott, Joyce McDermott and child, Catharine Fitzpatrick, Bridget Burke, Peggy Purky, John Belton, Mary Dolan, Thomas Fahey, Bridget Fahey, Martha Fahey, Honora Donnelly, Honora Mullen, sisters Catherine and ---Henniff, Mary Cahill,

Patrick Noonan, Mary Landsky, Meggy Mullen and her sister's child, and John Butler.

A Melancholy List
(Taken from a newspaper article printed in a paper whose name I do not know)

The Boston papers publish the following list of passengers who were lost by the wreck of the bark St. John's from Galway, Ireland, off Cohasset, on the 6th instant:

Cabin Passengers Lost – Mary Flannegan and Nancy Hannagan, Margaret Hannagan of Kilfenora, county of Clair; Bridget Quinn and Eliza O'Brien, of Inistivan, Claire.

Steerage Passengers Lost – Ann Slatterly, Bridget Slatterly, Hugh Maddigan, Margaret Keenan, of Inistivan; Bridget Connelly and 8 children, Patrick Sweeney and wife and 9 children, of Kannanara, county of Galway; Peter Greally and James Greally, of Claronbridge, county of Galway; Patrick Gorman, Miles Sweeney, Thomas Burke – mother saved – Eliza Burke, Patrick Burke, Misses McDermott – sisters – Mary Love and child, Catharine Fitzpatrick, Bridget Burke, Bridget Mulligan, Peggy Purky, Martha Puray, all of Galway; Michael Hannagan, Lalinch, county of Clare; Patrick Lahiff, John Lahiff, Thomas Riley, Bridget Maddigan, of Kilfenora, county of Clare; Hugh Glynn, of Inistivan, county of Clare; John Belton, Mary Dolan, Thos. Fahey, Bridget Fahey, Martha Fahey, Honora Donnelly, Honora Mullen, Catherine Heniff and ---- Heniff – sisters – Mary Cahill, Patrick Noonan, Mary Landskey, Peggy Mullin and sisters child, John Butler, of county Galway; Patrick McMahan, Bridget McMahan, Catherine McMahan, Mary Nalon, Mary Frowley and child, of Kilmaly, county of Clare; John Dolan, Roan, county of Clare; Mary Freeman and child, Mr. Egan, wife and daughter, Martin Sexton, of Innis, county of Clare; Jeremiah Murphy, James Moran, Dysant, county of Clare; Margaret Keenan, Miss Brooks, of Inistivan; Lant Byrnes, Michael Griffin, Cathrine Burns, Peggy Malloy, Ellen Hasset, of Anch, county of Clare; Patrick McGrath, James McGrath, Winny Galvin, Mary Galvin, Margaret Kane, Mary McNamara, of Kilmaly; Honora Lahiff,

*On Grampus Ledge*

of Roan, John Lahiff or Rohan, Mary Curtin, Honora Mulkenan, Mary Mulkenan, Margaret Mulkenan, of county of Clare.

Passengers saved – (taken from The Watertown Chronicle, Watertown, Wisconsin, Oct. 24, 1849) – Eleven of the crew and: Austin Kearn, C. Flanagan, Betsey Higgins, Mary Kane, M. Fitzpatrick, M. Gibbons, Barbara Kenely, M. Redding, H. Cullen, and Honora Burke.

Cabin Passengers Lost – (taken from The Watertown Chronicle, Watertown, Wisconsin, Oct. 24, 1849) – Of Kilfinara, Co. Clare: Mary Flannegan, Nancy Hannagan, and Margaret Hannagan.
Of Inistivan, Co. Clare: Bridget Quinn and Eliza O'Brien.

Steerage Passengers Lost – (taken from The Watertown Chronicle, Watertown, Wisconsin, Oct. 24, 1849) – Of Instivan: Ann Slattery, Bridget Slattery, Hugh Madigan, Margaret Keenan, Hugh Glynn, Margaret Keenan, and Miss Brooks.
Of Kannamara (Connemara), Co. Galway: Bridget Connelly and eight children, and Patrick Sweeney, his wife, and their nine children.
Of Claronbridge, Co. Galway: Peter and James Greally.
Of Galway, Co. Galway: Patrick Gorman, Miles Sweeney, Thomas Burke (mother saved), Eliza Burke, Patrick Burke, Mrs. McDermott (sisters), Mary love and child, Catharine Fitzpatrick, Bridget Burke, Bridget Mulligan, Peggy Purky, and Martha Puray.
Of Kilmaly, Co. Clare: Patrick McMahan, Bridget McMahan, Catharine McMahan, Mary Nalon, and Mary Frowley and child.
Of Lalinch, Co. Clare: Michael Hannagan.
Of Kilfanora, Co. Clare: Patrick Lahiff, John Lahiff, Thomas Riley, and Bridget Maddigan.
Of County Galway: John Belton, Mary Dolan, Thomas Fahey, Bridget Fahey, Honora Donnelly, Honora Mullen, Catherine and --- Henniff (sisters), Mary Cahill, Patrick Noonan, Mary Landskey, Peggy Mullin and sister's child, and John Butler.
Of Roan, Co. Clare: John Dolan.
Of Innis, Co. Clare: Mary Freeman and child, Mr. Egan, his wife, and daughter, and Martin Sexton.

Of Dysart, Co. Clare: Jeremiah Murphy, and James Moran.

Of Anch, Co. Clare: Daniel Byrnes, Michael Griffin, Catharine Burnes, Peggy Malloy, and Ellen Hasset.

Of Kilmaly, Co. Clare: Patrick McGrath, Winny Galvin, Mary Galvin, Margaret Kane, and Mary McNamara.

Of Rohan: Honora Lahiff.

Of County Clare: John Lahiff, Mary Mulkenan, and Margaret Mulkenan.

Passengers saved – (source unknown) – Austin Kearn (20), Betsey Higgins (21), Michael Fitzpatrick (26), Barbara Kennelly (20), Michael Redding (24), Honora Cullen (28; three children lost), Mary or Honora Burke (three children lost), Catharine Flannagan (20), Mary Kane (24), Michael Gibbon (26), and Mary Slattery (26).

Crew saved – (source unknown) – Captain [Martin] Oliver, 1st Mate Henry Cummerford, Henry O'Hern, Michael Kennelly, William Larkin, Isaac Cummerford, Thomas Walker, James Flaherty, and Andrew Forest.

Cabin Passengers Lost – (source unknown) – Of Kilnare, Co. Clare: Mary Flannigan, Nancy Hannagan, and Margaret Hannagan.

Of Inistivan, Co. Clare: Bridget Quinn and Eliza O'Brien.

Steerage Passengers Lost – (source unknown) – Of Innistivan, Co. Clare: Ann Slattery, Bridget Slattery, Hugh Madigan, Margaret Keenan, Hugh Glynn, Margaret Keenan, and Miss Brooks.

Of Lalinen, Co. Clare: Michael Hannagan.

Of Kilanara, Co. Clare: Patrick Lahiff, John Lahiff, Thomas Riley, and Bridget Maddigan.

Of Roan, Co. Clare: Patrick McMahan, Bridget McMahan, Catherine McMahan, Mary Nalon, and Mary Frowley and a child.

Of Innes, Co. Clare: Mary Freeman and child, Mr. Egan, his wife, and child.

Of Dyant, Co. Clare: Martin Sexton, Jeremiah Murphy, and James Moran.

Of Anch, Co. Clare: Daniel Byrnes, Michael Griffen, Catherine Burnes, Peggy Maloy, and Ellen Hasset.

Of Kilmary, Co. Clare: Patrick McGrath, James McGrath, Winny Galvin, Mary Galvin, Margaret Kane, and Mary McNamara.

Of Clare, Co. Clare: Honora Lahiff, or Rowan, John Lahiff, or Rowan, Mary Curtis, Honora, Mary, and Margaret Mulkenan.

Of Kunnamara, Co. Galway: Bridget Connelly, Patrick Sweeney, his wife, and nine children.

Of Galway, Co. Galway: Patrick Corman, Miles Sweeney, Thomas Burke, Eliza Burke, Mary McDermott, Joyce McDermott and child, Catherine Fitzpatrick, Bridget Burke, Peggy Purky, Martha Purky, John Belton, Mary Dolan, Thomas Fahey, Bridget Fahey, Martha Fahey, Honora Donnelly, Honora Mullen, Catherine Heniff and her sister, Mary Cahill, Patrick Noonan, Mary Landsky, Peggy Mullen and her sister's child, and John Butler.

From The Cohasset Town Records, found in the archives of the Cohasset Historical Society, the names of some of the deceased of the wreck of the St. John: Catharine Fitzgerald, Peggy Mullen and her sister's child, Bridget Mulligaw [sic], Bridget Burke, Peggy Purky, Sally Sweeney, John Dolan and his wife, Martha Perky, Patrick Sweeney, --- Lahiff (a female), Mary Freeman, and Mary Joice.

A newspaper article stated that Peggy Mullen, her child, and her own sister, perished in the wreck, but there is no record of that. Another article stated that Peggy Adams died in the wreck, but the only listing I found was for a sister.

And what of the passengers and crew that survived? Austin Kearin, or Kerrin, moved to Moretown, Vermont, and married Ellen Hasset; it is interesting to note that one of the passengers listed as deceased was an Ellen Hasset. Could this be the same woman? The couple would have nine children, and of their great-grandchildren, one, a woman, lives in Colorado today. In later years, his sister, Frances, would come to live with the couple.

According to the website, connemaraislesgolfclub.ie, "The clubhouse of this amazing course is the ancestral home of the Lynch Brothers: Cathal, John, and Tony. It was built in 1850 by their great-grandfather, a man named Flaherty. After surviving the wreck of the brig St. John, in 1849, the Brothers Flaherty returned to Ireland and built that ancestral home.

"James Flaherty returned to Lettermullen, married, and raised a family. Patrick Flaherty did the same. Martin Flaherty married a young lass from Annaghuane, a small village about 7 miles from Lettermullen. The brothers all had families and their descendants live in the area today."

Patrick "Paddy" Mulkerrins, of Lettermullen, Co. Galway, Ireland, states that Isaac Comerford, the ship's 1st Mate, stayed in America, joined the U. S. Navy, and served, honorably, as a surgeon.

There are numerous rumors swirling around the now dead and decaying body of Captain Oliver. For instance, what was his first name? Rumor has it that it was Martin, but that has never been verified. What we do know is this, after landing in Scituate, at the Glades, Oliver is suddenly in Boston, with his 1st Mate; after that I have no idea what happened to him.

Then one day in November, 1989 a man walked in to the Cohasset Historical Society, and the curator, David H. Wadsworth, recorded his story, and I quote.

"...Mr. Stephen Oliver, of...Hull, Massachusetts, visited Lothrop House to talk with the senior Curator. He brought with him a copy of [a] recent Patriot Ledger article relating to the 140th Anniversary program of the sinking of [the] brig St. John, held by the Cohasset Historical Society.

"He inquired as to the name 'Martin Oliver', given as the Captain of the St. John. [The] Curator explained that the name 'Martin' was not verified, but was given by a Mr. Joyce of Lettermullen, [County Galway, Ireland], as a possibility of having been that captain's first name, at [the] Maritime Museum several years ago. Mr. Oliver stated that, when he was a child his father had told him that his uncle (Mr. Oliver's great uncle) had been Captain of a famine ship from Galway which had crossed the Atlantic to Cape Cod and had been wrecked on the Massachusetts shore.

"The name of the ship was unknown to Stephen Oliver, but he now believes it must have been the St. John. He also noted that he is a relative of Paul St. John of Cohasset, who is his wife's sister's husband.

"Mr. Oliver did not know the first name of the captain referred to by his father. The first name of Captain Oliver of [the] St. John, unfortunately, remains unknown."

Where to begin? There are so many errors on each of the lists, or partial lists I have seen, that it actually boggles the mind. Whoever compiled each of these lists had a difficult time with the Clare and Galway accents. Others errors may have occurred during the typesetting, or at the printing stage. There are numerous errors in place names, numbers of people on the ship, and the names of those persons. So, we will start with what appears to be the easiest of these situations; the misspelling of place names.

Kilnare, Killanara, Kilfanara, Kilfanora, and Kilanara, are actually Kilfenora. The town of Ennistymon is spelled Innistivan, Inistivan, Issistivan, and Instivan. Anch, Lalinen, and Lalinch are actually Lahinch. Roan is actually Ruan, as is Rohan. Innes is really Ennis, as is Innis. Dysart is misspelled Dyant. Kilmary and Kilmaly are actually Kilmurry. Connemara is spelled as Kuhnanmar, Kunnamara, or Kannamara. Next, we look to the names of the passengers and crew for misspellings. The first group of misspellings comes when we examine the sisters Flanagan. The written "Fl" is misread by a typesetter as the capital letter H, so when you see the name Hannagan, in reference to these three sisters, the names should actually read Nancy, Mary and Margaret Flanagan. The Watertown Chronicle of Watertown, Wisconsin misspells Flanagan as Flannegan, also. An unknown source, possibly a reporter spells Flanagan as Flannigan.

From the list of passengers saved we find that Austin Kearin, has become Austin Kearn. Mary Kane is also, Margaret Kanan, Margaret Keenan, Margaret Kane, Mary Cane, or even Bridget Kane. Michael Gibbon is Michael Gibbons; Barbara Kennelly becomes Barbara Kenely; Honora Cullen is Honor Cullen, Honora Burke is Honor Burke, as well as Mary Burke. Among the crew saved, Andrew Frost becomes Andrew Forrest, and the Commerford's are called the Cummerfords.

*Paul A. Fiori*

From the list of passengers lost we find that Bridget Maddigan's name has also been spelled Bridget Madigan. The name Mary Nalon will be looked at, in depth, in the Letters and E-mail section of this book. Is John Belton really John Batton, or are they two different men? I assume that Catherine Burnes and Catherine Burns are the same person. Peggy Molloy is also called Peggy Malloy and Peggy Maloy. Patrick Sweeney and his wife, Catherine, are noted as the Swaney's on one list. The Mulkenan Sisters are really the Mulkennan Sisters, or is that vice versa? Peggy Mullen is also, Meggy Mullen, Peggy Mullin, and Peggy Miller. Patrick Gorman is also spelled Patrick Corman and Michael Cormaine. Peggy Purky becomes Peggy Purkey; Martha Purky is misspelled as Martha Puray. Miss Catherine Heniff has her name misspelled as Henif on one list, and her unnamed sister is named on one list as Mary Henif. Mary Landsky is called Mary Landskey on one list. It is difficult to ascertain with any accuracy which names are misspelled and which are not, all I can do is try my best to point out the errors.

Now comes the virtually impossible task of figuring out how many people; passengers and crew, were actually on board the St. John when she wrecked. In order to be as accurate as possible I will list each passenger individually with a corresponding number, in parentheses next to the name, to show how many lists that person appears on.

Passengers Saved: Austin Kearin (6), Catherine Flannagan (6), Betsy Higgins (6), Mary Keane (2), Mary Cane (1), Mary Kane (3), Michael Fitzpatrick (6), Michael Gibbon (6), Barbara Kennelly (6), Mary Slattery (5), Michael Redding (6), Honora Cullen (6), Honora Burke (6), and a Miss Quinlan (1). The list of the crew saved and the crew lost, are the same as earlier shown.

Now here is where it gets dicey! I will do my best to sort out the list of passengers lost. Note that there are more lists of passengers saved than those that were lost.

Passengers Lost: Mary Flannagan(4), Nancy Flannagan (4), Margaret Flannagan (4), Bridget Quinn (4), Eliza O'Brien (4), Ann

Slattery (3), Bridget Slattery (3), Hugh Madigan (3), Margaret Keenan (4?), Hugh Glynn (3), Margaret Keenan (4?), Miss Brooks (4), Michael Hannagan (3), Patrick Lahiff (3), John Lahiff (7), Thomas Riley (3), Bridget Maddigan (4), Bridget McMahon (3), Patrick McMahan (3), Catherine McMahan (3), Mary Nalon (3), Mary Frowley and child (3), The Cullen Children (6), Honora Burke's children (6),: Honora Cullen and Honora Burke each lost 3 children, for a total of six children lost.

Mary Freeman and child (5), Mr. Egan, his wife and daughter (3), Martin Sexton (3), Jeremiah Murphy (3), James Moran (3), Daniel Byrnes (3), Michael Griffen (3), Catherine Burnes (3), Peggy Molloy (3), Ellen Hasset (3), Patrick McGrath (3), James McGrath (2), Winny Galvin (3), Martin Galvin (3), Margaret Kane (3), Bridget Kane (1), Mary MacNamara (3), Honora Lahiff/Rohan/Rowan (3), Mary Curtis (2), Mary Curtain (1), Honora Mulkenan (3), Mary Mulkenan (4), Margaret Mulkenan (4), Bridget Connelly (3), Patrick Sweeney, his wife and 9-11 Children (5).

Patrick Corman (4), Miles Sweeney (3), Thomas Burke (3), Eliza Burke (3), Mary McDermott (2), Joyce McDermott and child (2), A Mrs. McDermott (2), Catharine Fitzpatrick (4), Bridget Burke (5), Peggy Purky (4), John Belton (3), John Batton (1), Mary Dolan (3), Thomas Fahey (3), Bridget Fahey (3), Martha Fahey (3), Honora Donnelly (3), Honora Mullen (4), Catherine and Mary Henniff (4 each), Mary Cahill(3), Patrick Noonan (3), Mary Landsky (3), Meggy Mullen and her sister's child (5), John Butler (3), Mary Love and her child (1), Peter and James Greally (1 apiece), Patrick Burke (1), Bridget Mulligan (2), Martha Purkey (2), John Dolan and his wife (3), Catherine Fitzgerald (1), Lahiffs; a female (1), Mary Joice and child (2), Michael Flanagan (1),

James Loheff (1), Nappy and Thomas Farley (1), Honora Quinlan (1), Mrs. Cornelia (1), Peggy Fahey and child (1), a servant girl (2), Bridget Kennelly and three children (1), Honora Donnelly (1), a woman and her eleven children (1), Honora and Thomas Lahey (1).

The Boston Post of October 10, 1849 stated, eleven passengers survived, nine of the crew survived, seven of the crew perished and eighty-two passengers were lost, for a total of 109 souls on board. Two days later, it revised that number and added nine more to its departed passengers list. The Watertown Chronicle of Watertown, Wisconsin has eleven crew surviving, eleven passengers surviving, seven crew as lost and ninety-six passengers as lost, for a total of 125 souls on board. Other totals I have seen are 109 dead, 22 survivors, for a total of 131 passengers on board.

The Alton Telegraph and Democratic Review has the total at 119 passengers and crew that had sailed; Thoreau has the total at 165 people on board; The Boston Journal of October 17, 1849, has the total at 164; The Burlington Hawkeye has the total at 175; other total I have seen, from unnamed sources are 157, 120, 114, and 150 passengers and crew on board the St. John when she wrecked.

Quote from an unknown source. "On this occasion, the fact that the brig had more passengers than she was licensed to carry attracted attention, as did the fact that Capt. Oliver and the majority of his crew survived, but only eight passengers did the same..."

Mary Kane! It is well-known that she survived the wreck, and that her name appears on six passenger lists as a survivor, but, she also appears on four lists of the deceased of the wreck. However, there are questions to be asked; is this woman also Mary Keane, Mary Cane, or Bridget Kane, or are they different women? Since Captain Oliver's original passenger manifest went down with the ship, plus the second, or alternate one, we will never know the answer.

Why does Mary Slattery appear on only five of the seven lists? Why is Mrs. Quinlan on two lists: 1 as dead, 1 as living? Why do some lists show seven crewmembers lost and others show nine? On one list of passengers saved ten names appear, on a second eleven names appear, and on a third twelve names appear. James Flaherty appears on the lists of the passengers saved, but his brothers Martin and Patrick are not on any of those lists. Were his brothers actually on the ship? Were they the two unnamed passengers in the lifeboat that landed safely at The Glades? Margaret Keenan appears on one list twice! Are they actually the same woman, or are they two different women? Are John Lahiff and John Loheff the same person? Are John Lahiff-Rowan and John Lahiff-Rohan the same person, or is Rowan/Rohan the town of Ruan? Mary Freeman appears on one list alone and on another as Mary Freeman and child. Ellen Hasset is on every list of passengers lost. It is interesting to note that Austin Kearin, one of the wreck's survivors, married an Ellen Hasset of Anch, Ireland (actually Lahinch, Ireland), the same town the deceased Miss Hasset came from.

Are Mary Curtis and Mary Curtain the same woman? Honora Mulkenan appears on three lists as deceased, along with her sisters. However, on one list, only her sisters names are recorded. Bridget Connelly appears on all the lists of the deceased, but on one list she appears as Bridget Connelly and her 8 children. Patrick Sweeney and his family are seen on every list of the deceased, that I have seen. On one list they appear as Patrick Sweeney, his wife, and 11 children (I have seen numbers from 9-11 for his children). On another list, they are noted as Patrick Sweeney, his wife and 9 children. On one list his wife's name appears separately, and on yet another list they are called the Swaney's.

One list has, next to the name Thomas Burke, the words "Mother saved; was she one of the survivors? There are no Burke's listed as surviving, except Honora Burke. Was this woman Thomas Burke's mother? If so, she is listed as having lost three children. Are John Batton, John Butler, and John Belton the same person? What does the word "sisters" mean next to Mrs. McDermott's name? Meggy Mullen is listed alone on one list, and as Meggy Mullen and her sister's child, on another. On some lists John Dolan is listed alone, on others, with his wife. Mary Joice is listed alone on one list, and with a child on another. Is Michael Flannagan actually Michael Hannagan, or vice versa? I have seen Peggy Adams as a survivor and a victim in stories about this wreck, I wonder which is true?

# APPENDIX C
## Interviews, Letters and E-mails

A letter from Paddy Mulkerrins to David Wadsworth of the Cohasset Historical Society, and reprinted here with the permission, of the Cohasset Historical Society, and I quote.

"Dear Mr. Wadsworth,
"Thank you for the copy of the article on the St. John, which I found very interesting; also the letter by that young girl on the St. John survivors, which I can add to my archives. Thank you.
"Further on the St. John. She was built in 1837. First Mate, Isaac Comerford was a surgeon. He remained in America and joined the U.S. Navy. That's all I have for you at this time. Take care and have a good X-mas.

Yours sincerely,
Paddy Mulkerrins

I found this in the Archives of the Cohasset Historical Society, and courtesy of the Cohasset Historical Society, reprint it here.
In an interview with William J. Loughran of the Eire Society of Boston, and published in its "Bulletin" of November 1987, Paddy Mulkerrins stated, and I quote. "I was born and raised on Lettermullen, and while growing up I heard many stories of…the St. John wreck… with the loss of so many young men and women from our part of Galway. Legend has grown…about the wreck…[Many] of the survivors came back to Ireland. With their terrible burden of sorrow, I think they

had come home to the comfort of friends and familiar surroundings… Some descendants of the survivors still live on Lettermullen.

"…The people of Lettermullen, and our part of Galway, deeply mourned the loss of so many lovely young girls and fine-looking young men…It was not the first ship wrecked on the Yankee shore, and it [wouldn't] be the last."

In a letter to the Cohasset Historical Society, Lt. Cmdr. Niall Brunicardi, wrote about a poem he'd seen published, by an Eileen M. Egan, of Fermoy, Ireland and Dorchester, Massachusetts. I add the letter here, courtesy of the Cohasset Historical Society, and I quote.

"Dear Sir,
"I enclose a copy of a poem by a Fermoy lady, Eileen M. Egan, regarding the wreck of the St. John, a full-rigged ship of 985 tons, Master Richardson, built at St. John, N.B, in 1844, owned by Owens and Company, of St. John, on a voyage with emigrants from Galway to Boston, in the year 1849, when it was wrecked, apparently on Minot's Ledge.

"Have you any information on the granite slab erected as a memorial? Is there a list of victims of the disaster? Who had the memorial erected? Were there any survivors?"

Yours Sincerely,

Niall Brunicardi

A letter from Miss Loretta Sullivan, of Lowell, Mass., to the Cohasset Historical Society, and reprinted here courtesy of the Cohasset Historical Society, and I quote.

"Gentlemen,
"Last week I had the opportunity to fulfill a life's dream when my sister and I were driven to a cemetery in Cohasset, to see the monument which was dedicated to the memory of the Irish immigrants who were shipwrecked off the coast of Cohasset, in 1848 (the year is actually 1849).

"My mother, who was born in Lowell, Mass. in 1867, often told us that her mother's sister (maybe there were 2 sisters) was lost at sea in a shipwreck off the coast of Scituate (we learned in later years the tragedy occurred off Cohasset, but it probably was the same range of rocks).

"Just last week a gentleman from Syracuse, New York drove my sister and I to see the monument which was [provided] by the Ancient Order of Hibernians, in 1914. We were very impressed.

"We were hoping against hope that the names of some of the passengers might be available somewhere (I suppose that if the ship was lost at sea, the list of passengers would be lost also).

"My mother was extremely young when her parents passed away, and she was brought [to America] by an aunt on her father's side of the family.

"If the ill-fated passenger on the St. John was not married, her name would have been NEILON, or NEYLON. But, if she were married I would have no idea what her name was.

"I do know that her Birthplace would have been County Clare, Ireland…"

Sincerely,
(Miss) Loretta Sullivan
Lowell, Mass.
July 23, 1978

On March 17, 2007, St. Patrick's Day, or, if you are a Waspish Bostonian, Evacuation Day, I received an e-mail from Patrick "Paddy" McGrath. I had been looking for information on the passengers and crew of the St. John, in this case the Brothers Flaherty: James, Martin and Patrick. I'd heard that relatives of the brothers still resided in Ireland; they were named Lynch. "Paddy" wrote in this e-mail, and the ones following, and I quote. "The John Lynch you are looking for lives in Leitirmore. He is the manager of the Bealedandan (sic) Golf Club. I think only one survivor stayed in the USA. She married a man named St. John...Slan, Paddy McGrath."

I sent "Paddy" an e-mail requesting any information that would put me in contact with John Lynch. The next day, March 18th, I received the following e-mail. "Hi Paul, John Lynch can be con[tacted] at John Lynch (I have chosen not to give out the address), Co. Galway, Ireland. You can use my name, he knows me fairly well. Sorry...don't have his tele no.,...Paddy McGrath."

In my next e-mail to him I inquired about the town of Anch, Co. Clare, Ireland, I told him about Mary Kane and James St. John, about Austin Kearin and Ellen Hasset, and about "Paddy" Mulkerins. He replied back a day later.

"The town is Lahinch, in Co. Clare. Most of the passengers on the brig St. John came from Co. Clare. I don't know much about the St. John. I knew "Paddy" Mulkerins many years ago. My neighbor, Jimmy Nee, his mother was a Flaherty from Lettermullen. Her brothers were on the St. John. Hope I'm of some help...Paddy McGrath."

I replied, "There were two McGrath's on the St. John, Michael and James, from Kilmary. Possible relations? Can you get the Nee address for me? If so, inform them I will be trying to contact them. I appreciate all of your help...Slan!"

"Paddy" wrote back. "Hi Paul, The Nee family I mentioned} are death(sic). The best man to talk to is John Connolly, Furnish, Lettermullen, Co. Galway. I met him a few years ago at the anniv. for the St. John. I'll try to get his tele no. The papers that time did not do a good job of getting the names and addresses of the pass..."Paddy": McGrath."

Paul A. Fiori

In my next e-mail to "Paddy", I asked him to translate a few words from English to Gaelic for me. "Paul, The Gaelic for Grampus Ledge is "leac an mor. I heard that Captain Oliver was not the original Captain on the St. John. The St. John was on the 2nd trip to New England and that Capt. Greene was sick…Slan, "Paddy" McGrath."

I next heard from "Paddy" on March 28th, when he gave me John Connolly's phone number…"Hope it's the right number. I got that no. from a friend of his sister' Maggie…Good Luck, "Paddy" McGrath."

On Easter Sunday, April 8, 2007, as I was about to pay for my breakfast, at The Silver Spoon Café, in Cohasset, who should walk in but Brendan St. John, the great-great-great grandson of James St. John, the Cohasset man who married Mary Kane. We discussed the wreck and his relatives briefly, then went our separate ways.

The next day I received an e-mail that read, "I was searching the Internet and couldn't help but stumble across your request for info on the Brig St. John. Mary Kane was one of the survivors who [happened] to marry my great-great-great grandfather. I am from Cohasset and most of my family lives there. I currently live in Boston. I'd be happy to help since we have lots of info on this. Let me know, Martin St. John."

How lucky can one get? To speak to two members of the St. John family within days of each other; this project is taking me to ports unknown. I immediately wrote to Martin, introduced myself, and my first question was about Captain Oliver. I am waiting for his reply.

On Saturday, April 4, 2007, I received an e-mail from Peter Beirne, of the Clare Library in County Clare, Ireland, and I quote. "Thank you for your postal letter to the Clare County Library, http:www.clarelibrary.ie/, enquiring about the brig…St. John wrecked off the Massachusetts coast in 1847(sic).

"I have a couple of items on file, which I will mail out to you by post on Monday 16 April. These duplicate materials in some of the links below. "As regards present relatives of survivors of the shipwreck who live in County Clare, I recommend you write a short letter to the publisher of the local newspaper "The Clare Champion" (see http: www.clarechampion.ie/CLCH/www/). He will publish your letter in the paper with your contact details and such relatives reading the letter will hopefully contact you themselves by phone, post or e-mail. Write to John Galvin. Publisher. The Clare Champion. Barrack Street, County Clare.

"I enclose some links from the Clare Library website, which might be of interest."

With best wishes,
Peter Beirne
County Clare Library

Date: Thursday, 3 April, 2008, and I quote.
"Paul,
"First of all, let me just say, your writing is fantastic. I'm flattered that you mentioned me in such an honorable light. I guess I owe my blood to none other than being born so I'm not sure I deserve it. Regarding the content, you've certainly done your research. My father always said it would make a great movie if it ever made it to film.

"Some of what you've written I had never read before so this has been particularly interesting to me. I wish I could add more but as I've been racking my brain for the past week, I can't see anything you have not covered. There is one ironic story that might be worth writing about so I'll mention it. You can choose whether it's worthy or not.

"Catherine Roche of Cohasset married Joseph St. John (James's son). Catherine's parents, John and Margaret Roche, lived in the cottage you now see on Pleasant Beach overlooking the Atlantic (after you go over the Atlantic Ave. causeway headed towards Hull, it is on your right). It had also served as a coot shooter's club at some point in its history. Joe and Catherine had six children, one of them, named Mary Elizabeth, was born on September 7, 1877, in Cohasset at the house on the Common. One unseasonably warm spring day, she went swimming at Pleasant Beach in front of her grandparents house Despite it being a warm day she caught a chill and developed pneumonia. She died only a few weeks later on May 27, 1894, at 17 years old. She died from the very same waters that her grandmother was able to survive in a shipwreck.

"It's a strange twist of fate, but I thought I'd mention it just in case. It's funny, I spend quite a bit of time sailing off Cohasset in the summer and often think of what that morning might have been like.

"Anyways, I think it's a great read and I think you progress is remarkable, considering all the info you've gathered. You have my e-mail…let's stay in touch."

Best – Martin St. John.

The Paul St. John Interview

What do we know about Mary Kane? Not much. Mary Kane is the only survivor that actually remained in Cohasset after the wreck. I knew that the St. John family of Cohasset were direct relatives of James St. John, the widower that Mary Kane married. So, I decided to interview, or at least set up a date, so I could interview Paul St. John, the patriarch of the family. I had already spoken to Mark, Brendan, and Martin St. John about the wreck, so an interview with Paul could only add to my research. It was a Thursday afternoon in September. I'd just finished talking to Sandy Carter, an old friend, about the drowning of Peter Grimes, which will be part of another book I am writing. As I was leaving I asked Sandy, "Where the hell does Paul St. John live?" He laughed and said "Right around the corner next to Julia Gleason, the house before hers." I smiled, thanked him, and drove to my destination. As I passed the house, I spotted Paul working in his front yard. Backing up, and then pulling in to the driveway, I parked, turned off my engine, got out of the car, and approached Mr. St. John.   "Hey Saint. How are you? It's Paul Fiori," I said nervously.   "He looked up from his chores, smiled, then said, "Paul, how are you?"

I replied that I was fine, and then said, "I was hoping to set up a day that I could come over to interview you for my book about the wreck of the St. John."

"Well, what's best for you?" he asked.

"Anytime really, I work nights, so any day is fine with me. Whatever is easiest for you is fine," I replied.

"How about giving me a call next week and we'll set it up for noontime any day you choose."

# On Grampus Ledge

Telling him that was perfectly fine with me, we shook hands and I headed back to my car, happy that he had agreed to the interview

I saw him again the following Tuesday. We spoke and agreed that the interview would take place on Thursday, the 25th of September. Knowing I had only two days to line up my questions, I walked away from Mr. St. John nervously, wondering if I could actually pull this off.

Well, it's Thursday the 25th, and I am nervous as hell. I have never, I repeat, never, conducted an interview, in my life. I'd prepared a list of questions, I just hoped they were the right ones. As I sat in my car in the parking lot of the Atlantica Restaurant on Cohasset Harbor, I puffed on one cigarette after another, watching the clock in my car, as it neared noontime. Noon. I decided to be fashionably late. I lit my last smoke, finished my coffee, and reread my questions. At 12:15, I headed over to the St. John residence.

As I took a seat in the St. John's parlor, I was nervous. After a bit of light banter, Mr. St. John's idea, which put me at ease, I asked my first question.

"What do you know about Mary Kane's life before the wreck?"

"Mary Kane remains, to this day, a woman of mystery. I do know she was married in Ireland, to a fellow named Cole. Her name was Mary Kane-Cole when she got here. Sadly, for her, he died in the Famine. I don't know how long they'd been married, but I don't think it was that long. When she got on that boat in Galway, she was all alone."

At this point Paul leaves the room for a moment and when he returns he has a video tape in his hand. "Watch this tape, it's about the St. John, it was made in Ireland. It'll really help you." I took the tape, gladly, and told him, "When I'm done with it I'll get it right back to you."

"So, after she comes ashore, alive, what happened to her?"

"There were twenty-two survivors, mostly the ships crew. From what my great-aunt Tess told me, she came ashore by Sandy Cove, near the old Lothrop House. She was probably brought to the Lothrop's House, and from there went to the Alms House, where the high school is today."

You know, there weren't too many Irish in Cohasset back then; probably only the St. John's and the Brennock's. The families had known each other up in Canada, New Brunswick, I think. They came to Cohasset at about the same time.

"Did she have a job before she met James St. John?

"I don't know. She may have been a domestic, or worked in one of the shops in the village. She may have worked for James St. John at one time.

"Old Saint would have been a good catch for any woman at the time. He owned a lot of land and houses you see. He owned the land where his shop stood on the Common, where the World War One Honor Roll is. Sold that land to the town for a buck I hear. It may have been one of his kids who sold it after he died; no matter, the town got it for a buck.

"They had a ten bedroom house where the real estate office is, at the corner of Stagecoach Way. He had a house on Pleasant Street, where Tom Anderson used to live, and another on Oak Street, where Bill O'Connell lived. I think the O'Connell's still own that house. My great-uncle sold them all for cheap. People used to say Old Saint was generous to a fault. He also owned the land where the rectory for St. Anthony's Church is; gave that land to the church for nothing.

"How long after the wreck did they meet?

"Like I said, she may have worked for him in his shop, and they met there. James St. John was born in 1812. He would marry Anastasia Powers, and the marriage would produce four off-spring: Margaret, Joseph, William, and John. Anastasia St. John died in 1853. In 1868, James St. John married Mary Kane-Cole, the daughter of Timothy and Mary Kane. He was 56 and she was about 42 or 43.

"He had his own kids, and there wasn't any Viagra back then, so they didn't have any kids. But his kids accepted her. As long as he was happy, the kids were happy for him. From all I know they had a very good marriage.

"James St. John passed away in 1894. The family plot is over in Hingham, at St. Paul's Cemetery. It's mostly a Catholic cemetery; all of the stones are Irish and Italian names. My son Gregory is buried there. Mary Kane is there too, but there is no stone marking her final resting spot.

"You see, there was no Catholic Cemetery in Cohasset back then, so Cohasset's Catholics were buried, for the most part, in St. Paul's.

*On Grampus Ledge*

I think Mary was first buried up at the cemetery at the Alms House, then moved to Woodside, and then to St. Paul's; at least that's what I've heard. St. Paul's Cemetery is on Hersey Street in Hingham."

Did she ever have any issues after the wreck, like psychological or drinking problems?

"No. But she was Irish, after all. She took a drink, but not to excess. The 'Irish Curse' you know.

"The people in town liked her, treated her nicely, for a Catholic. The day of the wreck, they acted like it was just another day, and the wreck was just something that happened; nothing more, nothing less.

"I guess most of the survivors went back to Ireland. Some moved elsewhere, but she was the only one that stayed in Cohasset.

"What about Captain Oliver?

'That asshole!" he blurted out. "What ever happened to the captain going down with his ship! He was one of the first into that lifeboat... and poof!...he was gone! He was a coward!" he said angrily.

"My wife's sister married a guy named Bob Oliver, and he always said he was related to the captain; I always doubted that though. He always wanted to go to the anniversary masses that are held every year; I always told him, if he was related to the captain, it wouldn't be right for him to go, so he never went.

"I remember the 150th Anniversary Mass, at St. Anthony's. Most of the time when that anniversary mass is held you're lucky to get a dozen people in the church. Well, at that 150th you couldn't find a seat in the church; people were actually lined up outside the church onto the sidewalks. People came from Cohasset, Boston, and Ireland that day, just to attend. It was a miserable day, too. Cloudy, raining, it was a downpour. And this Irishman; he'd come all the way from Ireland too, there was well over one hundred from Ireland there, this Irishman, he says to me, 'It's a fine mist of a day, isn't it?' Well, I just had to laugh.

"What about the Kathleen?"

"You know, the two Cohasset Lifeboats that went out never saw the St. John, but they did see the Kathleen. They went over to her, and got her crew and her few passengers off safely. Michael Brennock got a medal for that you know. The Kathleen eventually made it into Boston."

*Paul A. Fiori*

    Paul's final comments were, "You know, they teach the wreck of the St. John in school in Ireland; at least that's what I've heard. Wouldn't this story make a great movie?"

    A note from Paddy Mulkerrins to the Cohasset Historical Society regarding Ms. Egan's poem; "I came across the song in a local weekly paper. I thought you might like to add it to your St. John file." This poem first appeared in a magazine called, "Ireland's Own."

# APPENDIX D
## POEMS

# *The Disaster of the Emigrant Ship St. John*

Departed Galway in the Famine Year 1849; Wrecked on the American Shore
Courtesy of the Cohasset Historical Society

By Eileen M. Egan

She sailed from a land where the skies were dark,
With famine and despair.
And her prow was turned to a better world
And nobody had a care.

Though the sky was dark and the sea was rough
In their hearts was the steadfast glow
Of faith, when these Irish pilgrims sailed
One hundred years ago.

As Galway dimmed and disappeared
In the sunset's fading light
Their prayers went out across the sea
And were swallowed in the night.

Then they turned their faces toward the west
And as night wore on
These men and women, and children too
Aboard the good St. John
Saw visions in the stars that sped
Above them in the sky
Of Freedom in another land
And so the night went on.

Through days and nights that followed it

The good St, John could tell
How she bore these pilgrims safely on
And bore their dreams as well.

But destiny was riding too
And on that fateful day
She let them glimpse their promised land
Then drowned with ocean spray.
The hopes that never came to life,
The dreams they'd dream no more,
She gave their bodies to the sea
There on Cohasset shore.

Today there is a granite slab
Raised to their memories.
And out on Minot's Ledge at night
Waves ruffled by a breeze.

Still here within their deaths the sound
Of voices dead and gone
They are the dreams that would not die
The hopes that must go on
And find their place beyond the storm
Where past and present blend
For though men die, their dreams endure
Their vision never ends.

# *The Brig St. John*
## *By Arthur Tobin Brodeur*

Courtesy of the Cohasset Historical Society

They left the port of Galway
On a moonlit night,
For Boston they were bound.
In a stormy sea with land in sight
The St. John went aground.

Cries of anguish filled the air,
As waves washed families overboard.
They had no time for prayer.

Patrick Sweeney, and all his family
Drowned that fateful night.
The McMahon family perished too,
But not without a fight.

God called them all to heaven,
Ninety-nine met their Maker,
On that day,
On the rocks off Cohasset's shore,
Not far from the sheltered bay.
The St. John broke in two,
The waves washed all away,
Woe, she was no more.

When by morning light
They counted those that were alive,
Such a pitiful few,
And all the dead, who in Life met Death,
And Death had won.

Now, not one will see the morning sun.
The Irishmen and Irish women,
And their children,
Remember them we will.

For the Celtic Cross
Placed upon a hill,
Is a reminder that,
In the year of 1849
That the St. John sank into the sea,
Taking a total of 99.

# *After One Hundred Years*
## *By Marie S. Barnes*

Courtesy of the Cohasset Historical Society

Prologue
The Spirit Speaks

Out of the pages of hist'ry
Out of the dim, distant past,
Comes to me now a vision
Complete from the first to the last.

For I am a Spirit – Survivor –
Of one who died in the sea.
I am one from an ill-fated vessel,
A victim of Fate's stern decree.

What think I as I stand here
At this granite shaft – this shrine –
And read the names here engraven,
Names of neighbors, old friends of mine?

I think of the bright, happy dreamings,
The courage of venturing men,
The plans for future beginnings,
The things that might have been;
The strong hearts, scarcely regretting
The leaving of loved ones behind;
All filled with the zest of adventure,
With clear and new pictures in mind.
Here ye rest, my fellow voyagers,
In the land your feet ne'er trod.
Here your bodies found no haven,
While your spirits went to God.

# The Departure of the Brig St. John

Brightly the trav'lers were smiling,
Joyous their laughter rang,
Many the voices uplifted,
Carefree and happy they sang.
For were they not departing
To a fairer, brighter life?
Was not theirs to be, for the seeking,
An existence free from strife?

With rails bulging, with flags flying
The old, time worn brig, St. John,
Left her dock at Galway, Ireland,
On a bright September morn,
Just a hundred years ago now.
On her sailed an eager band
Of voyagers, facing westward
Toward a new life – in a new land.
Great their hopes and bright their planning;
Friends would greet them over there;
And new homes – new ties to be builded;
Fortunes made, and prospects fair.
Some aboard had strange forbodings
(This few survivors told)
For they knew the ship was rotting,
Timbers, planks, and rigging old.
She had long seen active service,
Shipping coal across the sea.
Now, with human freight, she journeyed
Toward the great Land of the Free.
But the younger folk, less knowing,
Threw away all thoughts of gloom,
Talked and planned the golden future,
Never dreamed of sudden doom.

# The Storm off Grampus Ledge

Long the voyage and uneventful
'Til the day they neared the land
When – upon them – came a tempest
As if hurled by mighty hand.
Old and weak, the vessel staggered
All her timbers twisted and groaned.
And her sails were torn into ribbons.
Wild the gale – as it blustered and moaned.
Off her course the ship soon floundered
A prey to the winds and the sea:
The helpless sport of the waters –
Only one outcome could there be.
All too soon the breakers engulfed her,
Then she hit Grampus Ledge – and stuck fast,
She was pounded and broken like tinder,
All on board to the wild waves were cast.

Survivors, historians, writers
Have better related the tale
Of panic and wild, frantic efforts
Of the fury and rage of the gale;
Of the screams of women and children;
Of the boats, capsizing and gone;
Of the few who were clinging to wreckage;
Of the doom of the old brig, St. John.
'Twas cruelly tragic – ironic –
That the voyage, which so nearly was o'er
Should end, in this awful disaster,
Almost within reach if the shore.
From the seven score souls who sailed on her,
So happy – so hopeful – a band
'Twas only a pitiful remnant
Of survivors who ever reached land.

# Searchers on the Cohasset Shore

Cohasset shores, the next morning,
When receded the waves and the tide,
Lay strewn with fragments of wreckage
And many human bodies beside.
While loved ones with hearts that were breaking
A desperate, sad, somber lot
Were searching for friend or dear one –
Or worse, were finding them not.
One mother, seeking her baby,
Who, in care of a sister, had sailed
Found both – their bodies together –
And her two fold bereavement bewailed.

# The Memorial Monument

Set on a knoll at harbor's edge
In our fair Cohasset town,
A shaft points ever skyward
With names, and dates set down.
The names of those who perished
One hundred years ago
Cut off in midst of all their dreams
By the sea – a merciless foe.
.

# Epilogue

## We Question the Spirit

What think ye, as ye stand there
Where rise this shaft of stone?
Ye Spirit of the bygone day
As ye stand apart and alone?
Think ye of all the visions
Of happy futures bright?
The dreams and hopes of fellow men
Facing the land of light?
See ye those friends and neighbors
Who, with you, the long voyage did face
Never to step on Earth's soil again,
Never that new life to embrace?
Not theirs the homes, the loved ones
For them, hopes blasted and gone
What think ye, oh Spirit – survivor –
As ye stand there alone?

# *God's Plan*

The Past lies silent in its shroud –
The Present glows and gleams.
What is the purpose of it all –
Those past and Present dreams?
What means Life's glories or its gains?
Of its tragedies – what worth?
Time blends all in Eternal plans –
Time blends, with Heaven, the Earth.
Know ye, who mortal art,
The Past – the Present – and the New
Are, of God's Plan a part?
So dream your dreams: see visions!
Go forth where none have trod!
Live ever with this watchword,
"For Country, and for God.

# Lost Souls
## By Mairian Ui Cheide

How calm was the ocean as it flirts with the shore,
The waves softly teasing with the gentle ebb and flow,
While the birdsong and wind, in hours reply,
The glorious enchantment of a fine October day.

But in this Cohasset graveyard lies a stone I'll unfold,
Of a wind so wild with fury and that true nor'easter roar,
That churned up the ocean and hurled waves with all its might,
At these poor hungry mortals that passed by one dark night.

They left their own familiar shore with the summer's sweet farewell
Their spirits nearly broken, all fears must be dispelled (quelled)
Hope was their saving; Faith was their grace,
As they sailed towards the New World with tears on their face.

And evil is the nation that drove Sweeney from his land
Who with all his toil and labor fed their mighty and grand
While his poor and hungry family wailed a woeful chant
As ships were being laden with grain, beef and ham

In sorrow and anger, you made your way to Galway bay
A last cry of anguish at your own true love's grave
Now motherless your children, one a babe in arms
One last fond glance at your native land as you all board the St. John.

On this ship built for cargo you crowded down below deck
Those with a few more farthings stay in cabins to rest
You prayed in the darkness and sang songs inside your head

As you viewed the far horizon and the promises it held.

In Cohasset Bay at the end of the day, the storm arose without warning.
The ship embattled by the wind lost its anchor, mast and rigging
Battered, shattered on Grampus Ledge, the Brig St. John met her death
Angels ferried the perished souls, left a handful to tell the story.

This graveyard tells the tale of a great Irish race
Whose courage we will proclaim through endless days
A cross that stands so tall it is seen from near and far
Everlasting as the memory of those who sailed on the Brig St. John.

The Voice would have the final word. "It has been 160 years since that most tragic of days. The waters off Cohasset still stir angrily whenever the nor-easters of winter batter this coast.

"The lifeboats at Whitehead are now a part of history, yet the beach where it was stationed, and where a few us found a saving hand still remains, as rock strewn as it ever was.

"Sandy Cove, where some of the living and the dead washed to shore, has changed a great deal. It is smaller now, the sands of time having crawled up onto its beach, covering what rocks were once there, and making it a most pleasant place. Many died on those rocks after drifting in to shore; those rocks battered our bodies again and again as we were being played by the tide. Yet no matter how much time has changed some things, others remain unchanged.

"Grampus Ledge still remains, as solid and dangerous as it ever was. That ledge has claimed more ships and many more lives, and may continue to do so in the future.

"Relatives of James St. John, the Cohasset businessman that married our Mary Kane, still reside in town. The waters off this coast have claimed one of that family also.

"The Celtic Cross, our memorial, has stood, firmly, since 1914. Every year since its erection, a memorial Mass is said in St. Anthony's

Church, the Catholic parish in town, and folks gather in the Joy Place Cemetery, to lay flowers and wreaths at our shrine, in memory of all who lived or died that October day.

"Our grave, the actual spot where we were buried, remains unmarked, even though its exact location is known to a few. We have not been forgotten; nor will we ever be. Yet, our spirits float, and always will, until the day that our now decayed bones are dug up and given another burial, a proper burial; perhaps under the Cross. It is said that the spirit never rests until its grave has been properly marked. Until that day, we float…"

Printed in the United States
218852BV00001B/12/P